Reading the Parables

INTERPRETATION

Resources for the Use of Scripture in the Church

INTERPRETATION

RESOURCES FOR THE USE OF SCRIPTURE IN THE CHURCH

Patrick D. Miller, *Series Editor*
Ellen F. Davis, *Associate Editor*
Richard B. Hays, *Associate Editor*
James L. Mays, *Consulting Editor*

OTHER AVAILABLE BOOKS IN THE SERIES

Ronald P. Byars, *The Sacraments in Biblical Perspective*
Jerome F. D. Creach, *Violence in Scripture*
Robert W. Jenson, *Canon and Creed*
Patrick D. Miller, *The Ten Commandments*

RICHARD LISCHER

Reading the Parables

INTERPRETATION *Resources for the Use of
Scripture in the Church*

WESTMINSTER
JOHN KNOX PRESS
LOUISVILLE · KENTUCKY

First edition
Published by Westminster John Knox Press
Louisville, Kentucky

14 15 16 17 18 19 20 21 22 23—10 9 8 7 6 5 4 3 2 1

Book design by Drew Stevens
Cover design by designpointinc.com

Library of Congress Cataloging-in-Publication Data

Lischer, Richard.
  Reading the parables / Richard Lischer.—First edition.
      pages cm—(Interpretation: resources for the use of scripture in the church)
  Includes bibliographical references and indexes.
  ISBN 978-0-664-23165-1 (hardback)
  1. Jesus Christ—Parables. I. Title.
  BT375.3.L56 2014
  226.8'06—dc23
                                                                    2014001707

♾ The paper used in this publication meets the minimum requirements of the American National Standard for Information Sciences—Permanence of Paper for Printed Library Materials, ANSI Z39.48-1992

Westminster John Knox Press advocates the responsible use of our natural resources. The text paper of this book is made from 30% post-consumer waste.

To Luke and Calvin

A certain man had two terrific grandsons . . .

CONTENTS

SERIES FOREWORD

This series of volumes supplements Interpretation: A Bible Commentary for Teaching and Preaching. The commentary series offers an exposition of the books of the Bible written for those who teach, preach, and study the Bible in the community of faith. This new series is addressed to the same audience and serves a similar purpose, providing additional resources for the interpretation of Scripture, but now dealing with features, themes, and issues significant for the whole rather than with individual books.

The Bible is composed of separate books. Its composition naturally has led its interpreters to address particular books. But there are other ways to approach the interpretation of the Bible that respond to other characteristics and features of the Scriptures. These other entries to the task of interpretation provide contexts, overviews, and perspectives that complement the book-by-book approach and discern dimensions of the Scriptures that the commentary design may not adequately explore.

The Bible as used in the Christian community is not only a collection of books but also itself a book that has a unity and coherence important to its meaning. Some volumes in this new series will deal with this canonical wholeness and seek to provide a wider context for the interpretation of individual books as well as a comprehensive theological perspective that reading single books does not provide.

Other volumes in the series will examine particular texts, like the Ten Commandments, the Lord's Prayer, and the Sermon on the Mount, texts that have played such an important role in the faith and life of the Christian community that they constitute orienting foci for the understanding and use of Scripture.

A further concern of the series will be to consider important and often difficult topics, addressed at many different places in the books of the canon, that are of recurrent interest and concern to the church in its dependence on Scripture for faith and life. So the series will include volumes dealing with such topics as eschatology, women, wealth, and violence.

The books of the Bible are constituted from a variety of kinds of literature such as narrative, laws, hymns and prayers, letters, parables, miracle stories. To recognize and discern the contribution and importance of all these different kinds of material enriches and enlightens the use of Scripture. Volumes in the series will provide help in the interpretation of Scripture's literary forms and genres.

The liturgy and practices of the gathered church are anchored in Scripture, as with the sacraments observed and the creeds recited. So another entry to the task of discerning the meaning and significance of biblical texts explored in this series is the relation between the liturgy of the church and the Scriptures.

Finally, there is certain ancient literature, such as the Apocrypha and the noncanonical gospels, that constitutes an important context to the interpretation of Scripture itself. Consequently, this series will provide volumes that offer guidance in understanding such writings and explore their significance for the interpretation of the Protestant canon.

The volumes in this second series of Interpretation deal with these important entries into the interpretation of the Bible. Together with the commentaries, they compose a library of resources for those who interpret Scripture as members of the community of faith. Each of them can be used independently for its own significant addition to the resources for the study of Scripture. But all of them intersect the commentaries in various ways and provide an important context for their use. The authors of these volumes are biblical scholars and theologians who are committed to the service of interpreting the Scriptures in and for the church. The editors and authors hope that the addition of this series to the commentaries will provide a major contribution to the vitality and richness of biblical interpretation in the church.

The Editors

ACKNOWLEDGMENTS

I owe much to the wisdom of my editors, Patrick Miller, Richard Hays, and Ellen Davis. They supported my research and writing with their technical advice, encouragement and, most generously, their patience. I will always be grateful to them.

Two research assistants, both generously supported by grants from Duke Divinity School, helped me bring this book to completion. Samantha Fong sifted through scores of books and articles on the parables of Jesus and offered excellent critical suggestions. Adam Barnard rendered invaluable assistance in organizing and formatting the bibliography for this book.

I have benefited from the teaching of too many scholars to enumerate them here. Their names may be found in the bibliography, though I do not consider them names only, but teachers, mentors, and partners who over the years have opened my eyes to the manifold mysteries of Jesus' parables. One name I must mention, however, and that is my friend and former colleague at Duke, Dan O. Via, whose work on the literary aspects of the parables ranks among the most important in the history of parable interpretation. Dan Via has shaped my thinking far more than the few formal references I have made to his seminal book, *The Parables: Their Literary and Existential Dimension*, would indicate.

For the past twenty years, and under a variety of titles, I have taught an elective course on preaching and the parables. For this book I have occasionally drawn on the insights of my students, along with memories of sermons preached, questions asked, and informal discussions that continued after class in other places. In many ways, this book represents a continuation of those wonderful conversations.

The reader will notice that in naming the parables I have adhered to traditional titles. I realize that the title plays a role in determining the interpretation of the parable, but any new or revised label, such as "The *Shrewd* Steward" or "The Prodigal *Father*," prejudices the interpretation no less than the old. The custom of using the first sentence or phrase of the parable as its title, for example, "A Man Casts Seed" or "The Land of a Rich Man," is a possibility, but one that tells the reader too little of what to expect. Moreover, the use of the initial phrase presupposes agreement among scholars as to the beginning and ending boundaries of each parable. Thus I have concluded that retaining the traditional titles will cause the least trouble for me and the reader.

Unless otherwise indicated, biblical quotations are from the New Revised Standard Version. What it sometimes lacks in traditional resonances and literary merit it makes up with inclusiveness and clarity.

Finally, I have dedicated this volume to my two grandsons, Luke and Calvin, aged twelve and eight, who with their mother's guidance have read the parables, received them in faith, and entered the kingdom of God as we all must, as children.

Richard Lischer
Duke Divinity School
Easter 2013

CHAPTER 1

A Preface to Reading the Parables

Søren Kierkegaard tells the story of a king who issued a royal command to everyone in his realm. His message, however, produced an unexpected response from his subjects. Instead of endeavoring to obey the command, they all became interpreters of it. Soon a prodigious body of criticism captured the imagination of all the people, who became fierce partisans of this or that critical position. Everything had become interpretation, but no one paid the least attention to the royal command. The king was willing to forgive his subjects everything—except their mistaken notion of what is truly important!

Kierkegaard frames his parable with the question, "What is the difference between criticism of a text and radical accountability to it?" (*Parables*, 12–13). The question contains its own answer. It is a warning to anyone foolish enough to engage in critical reflection on the parables of Jesus.

This is a book about reading the parables in such a way that we are held accountable by them. Although the title of the series in which this book appears is Interpretation, I prefer *Reading* because that is actually what we do with the parables. The word "reading" is a reminder that any piece of literature, including a parable, is not defined by its source, transmission, or the history of its interpretation, but by a text on the surface of a smooth page that lies across the lap. "Interpretation" ties the average person into knots. The

1

very word implies expertise, finality, and a critical position that has been staked out and must be defended. "Reading" gives us breathing space. It reminds us that no parable of Jesus has ever found its definitive, unassailable interpretation. In what follows we will examine several ways of reading the parables, not in the disinterested spirit of relativism, as if to claim that each reading is as true and makes as much sense as the next, but reading, first, as the primal interaction with a written document, and second, as the discriminating appreciation of *all* the dimensions of the text, including the historical, theological, literary, and sociopolitical.

If this book has a methodological premise, it is both medieval and postmodern in nature: no parable can be limited to one exclusive meaning, nor to a meaning that is unrelated to the milieu in which it has originated or the situation of those who read it. Reading begins with listening carefully to the text and allowing oneself to be perplexed by it. Reading comes in a flood of perceptions, including mixed and simultaneous messages, as well as echoes from other literature and from one's own experience. A community reads together in order to "get it right"—not necessarily in an academic sense, but for the sake of its common life and mission. Kierkegaard's warning speaks to everyone in the church but especially to those who write books for the church. We who balance our lives between church and academy know how easy it is to defer obedience to the word until we have surveyed every interesting interpretation of it.

In what follows, the reader will notice more than a few references to sermons preached on the parables of Jesus. This is because among Christians, as among the rabbis, the sermon quickly became the vehicle of the parable's interpretation and the locus of its authority. Unlike ancient sagas and ballads that were orally performed for millennia, the substance of the parables was "frozen" in circulating documents that were fast-tracked to the status of Christian Scripture. The church's roving prophets and balladeers did not long enjoy the freedom of performing the parables in ever-evolving mutations. What the church lost in the process of canonization, however, its preachers and biblical commentators gained in the creative freedom with which they interpreted the parables as texts. The parables found their home in the worshiping assembly, where preachers interpreted them and audiences endeavored to understand and live them.

2

The parables of Jesus are fictional stories. They are what Aristotle would have called "poetry," for which he claimed a higher seriousness than "history," since the historic is limited to what *has* happened, but the poetic is free to explore what *might* happen and is therefore more universal in nature (*Poetics* 1.9). The parables of Jesus belong to a category for which Aristotle did not have a name: theopoiesis (Greek *theopoiēsis*), the creative interplay of theological witness and poetic imagination (Wilder, *Theopoetic*, 1–12). *Poiēsis* is Greek for the act of "making." The first maker/poet is God, who, by means of the imaginative gifts of Jesus, crafted artifacts and performances of the divine presence in the world, much in the way a novelist "makes up" a set of characters, a plot, and setting in order to say something true and profound about human behavior. The second maker of a parable is the reader, who makes the internal assessments necessary to engage the story, allows it to speak, and makes a new home for it in the soul and the community. We do not read a parable in order to reduce it to a "lesson" any more than we would summarize a novel or a poem in a single sentence. Literature does not work that way. Moreover, churchgoers know that the elasticity of the parable is such that it can be preached from different perspectives and to different ends on successive Sundays. They also know that since a parable is a story to be told, its interpretation cannot be claimed as the exclusive province of the scholar but best emerges from its performance. The most effective teller of parables is not always the most educated preacher in town, for parables have a way of seeking out narrators with gifts and powers appropriate to their nature.

A parable communicates the most when it is read bifocally from within the heart of a religious community by believers who live fully in the world. For them, the parable serves as a bridge between the sacred life of faith and their duties and experiences in a secular world. As I hope to show in this book, the parables of Jesus are best read in constant conversation with the world and its many forms of literature. They belong to the world because in some measure they belong to human nature. They may even be called "worldly" or "secular"; for God loves the world depicted in them with a vividness and a humanity that only Jesus could fully express. The last three chapters of this book will explore the theological, literary, and sociopolitical dimensions of that worldliness.

3

The Problem

One of the first things we notice about parables is how rare they have become in our day. These tiny, stylized narratives have all but disappeared from the secular world as we know it. In politics, law, business, media, and ordinary conversation, the parable is largely absent from contemporary discourse. Its scarcity offers the first clue to its true character. It is a strange and difficult word—an *other* word—and, like the *other* race, language, accent, or worldview, the parable sounds a dissonant tone.

Imagine a press conference. An official of the World Bank has just been asked to comment on the worldwide debt crisis. She responds, "There was once a slave who owed his master one hundred million dollars. . . ." Or the chairman of the Federal Reserve, reflecting on the nation's economic prospects, muses, "A sower went out to sow."

Most scientists would not explain their painstaking devotion to research by querying, "Which one of you, having a hundred sheep and losing one of them . . ." And psychologists have another, more clinical word for the failure-to-launch, adult child who says resentfully, "You have never given *me* a young goat so that I might celebrate with *my* friends."

Parables can be notoriously puzzling to the average reader, since by definition a parable is a story whose meaning is rarely transparent and whose origins are often obscure. But it is not merely their opacity that has led to the disappearance of parables from our everyday language. It is something else. Mark Twain once said it wasn't the passages in the Bible that he could *not* understand that bothered him; it was the parts he understood all too well. Take Matthew 18:23–35, for example. As they contemplate the economies of Africa, the financial leaders of the developed world are more than capable of understanding Jesus' parable of the Unforgiving Slave. The first servant in Jesus' parable has been released from a huge, unrepayable debt by the powerful king. In turn, he refuses to forgive the tiny debt incurred by his fellow servant, for which he, the first servant, is roundly condemned by the Lord. In the context of the crushing debt load borne by the poorest countries, who among the powerful nations of the world, which have been given so much, could fail to understand the simple metrics of forgiveness in this little story? Thus from the beginning of our study, we must recognize that resistance to the parables of Jesus is not due to a lack of understanding. It proceeds from something deeper and harder to cure.

When considering the parables of Jesus, the reader faces an additional difficulty. Unlike other stories from antiquity, the parables of Jesus are integrally related to the character and mission of their teller. One can enjoy an Aesopian fable or a rabbinic story without much biographical or contextual background. The parables of Jesus, on the other hand, do not stand alone as individual stories but are woven into a larger narrative. In the Synoptic Gospels, the parables constitute approximately 35 percent of everything Jesus is reported to have said. In Luke, the figure rises to 52 percent, and in Matthew 43 percent (Snodgrass, *Stories with Intent*, 22). The earliest written account of Jesus' ministry, the Gospel of Mark, attests to their centrality: "He did not speak to them except in parables" (4:34a), which, as we shall learn, covers a broad range of figurative and poetic language. This means that what is often treated as a specialization by New Testament scholars might legitimately claim the lion's share of research on the spoken message of Jesus. It also means that the believer's investment in the parables runs deeper than the ordinary critic's, for the parables offer verbal evidences of Jesus' identity, message, and saving purpose in the world. Indeed, the most influential modern scholar of the parables, Joachim Jeremias, is convinced that in the parables of Jesus we are confronted by a unique and particularly trustworthy tradition. On the basis of stylistic and historical criteria, he asserts, "We stand right before Jesus when reading his parables" (*Parables of Jesus*, 12). To interpret a parable is to meet Jesus.

But interpretation is a circle. If the parables shed light on Jesus, the Synoptic Gospels' story of Jesus guides our interpretation of the parables. Two questions circle around and complete each another: How are we to relate these little stories to the figure of Jesus? How are we to compare what we know about Jesus to the distinctive stories attributed to him? Are the parables the gnomic utterances of a wandering teacher of wisdom? The coded ideology of a political and religious reformer? Or the veiled predictions of an apocalyptic seer? These options and many others are substantially represented in the tradition of parable interpretation. In our own day, followers of Jesus ask a simpler but more existential question: How are we to relate *our* prosaic lives and the parable-free zones in which we

5

live to the one who found this alien, *other* word indispensable to his ministry?

A second set of problems presents itself to modern interpreters. At first glance, the parable is *not* alien to us at all, or not as alien as it should be. When condensed into an aphorism, the parable plays a conserving function in all civilizations and cultures, embalming the practical wisdom of generations. Recently, the president of the United States warned that his opponent's economic plan was a case of "building on sand," and everyone knew what he meant without the citation of Matthew 7:26. Sometimes the parable form lends itself to a faux profundity, as in the brilliant satirical film *Being There* (1979), based on the novel by Jerzy Kosinski (1970). In it an illiterate gardener named "Chance" (played by Peter Sellers) is mistaken for an economic genius named Chauncey Gardner. His parabolic utterances are received as economic wisdom by the White House, Wall Street, and the media:

> PRESIDENT: Mr. Gardner, do you agree with Ben, or do you think that we can stimulate growth through temporary incentives? [*Long pause*]
> CHANCE: As long as the roots are not severed, all is well. And all will be well in the garden. . . . In the garden, growth has it seasons. First comes spring and summer, but then we have fall and winter. And then we get spring and summer again.
> BENJAMIN: I think what our insightful young friend is saying is that we welcome the inevitable seasons of nature, but we're upset by the seasons of our economy.
> CHANCE: Yes! There will be growth in the spring!
> BENJAMIN: Hmm!

The parables have been around a long time, but a comfortable familiarity does not breed understanding. A highly attenuated Christian culture has detached the better-known parables from their moorings in the life and ministry of Jesus and reduced them to a few bullet points of common sense. With their narrative strangeness gone, their punch lines are well known and approved by all. Everyone knows what a Good Samaritan or a Prodigal is. There is no need to rehash the stories or reacquaint ourselves with their context in the Gospel of Luke.

6

The tendency to simplify is not new or characteristic of our era alone. In the nineteenth century Adolf Jülicher opposed the church's allegorical method by insisting that each parable is a simple, straightforward story with but one point, which he called the *tertium comparationis*, the point of comparison. The *tertium* is the "third thing" which unites the abstract religious idea and the vivid picture contained in the parable. The problem with Jülicher's magisterial (and still untranslated) book on the parables, *Die Gleichnisreden Jesu*, is that the single "points" he substituted for the church's florid allegories tended to be universal maxims or truisms of the lowest common denominator. For example, the parable of the Talents reminds us that a reward must be earned by performance. The parable of the Dishonest Steward enjoins the wise use of the present as the condition of a happy future. The parable of Lazarus and the Rich Man teaches joy in a life of suffering and fear of a life of pleasure. The Good Samaritan represents the ideal of the neighbor (Greek *plēsion*), who is above all a fellow human being (*Gleichnisreden Jesu*, 485, 511, 634–35, 596; cf. Stein, *Introduction to the Parables*, 53–56). In his reading, Jesus' lessons tended to confirm what enlightened moderns already believed. The generic approach prompted the British scholar C. W. F. Smith's famous one-liner: "No one would crucify a teacher who told pleasant stories to enforce prudential morality" (*Jesus of the Parables*, 17).

One can assume that Jesus and his followers told and retold the parables many times and in a variety of circumstances. Unlike ancient performances of Homer, however, for the most part the parables were not recited in succeeding centuries but read from a uniform text and preached upon. Every sermon on a parable is a performance of a performance whose oral matrix and variability have been lost to us. The interaction of the spoken word with the later, written text produces at most a residual "voice" that can be heard only if one listens closely for it (cf. Ong, *Orality and Literacy*, 11, 31). One thinks of the disjunction between the immediacy of God's speaking in the Old Testament and God's subsequent command to write a book. Increasingly, the voice takes up residence in the book and in the prophet's interpretation of it (cf. Exod. 17:14).

The parables of Jesus arrive at our door as *texts* bound in a holy book. They are frozen transparencies of a ministry so dynamic that it was defined by dialogue and conflict until it was terminated in death. When Jesus told a parable, his voice occupied a particular

7

register; his facial expression undoubtedly matched his vocal into-
nation. He might have looked to the sky or to his Father above as
he told the story, as if to invoke the precise word he was looking for.
We suspect he may have laughed a little more heartily at his own
jokes than did his perplexed audience. His interlocutors must have
looked a bit uneasily or perhaps angrily at one another as these
stories sliced through their religious pretensions. Surely they raised
salient questions and objections, only a few of which we have on
record in the Gospels.

The real challenge to the modern imagination is not decipher-
ing the meaning of a particular parable, but again inhabiting an oral
world in which voice, memory, performance, and repetition are the
working tools of communication. In its spoken form, the parable
functioned in a rhetorical ecosystem of multiple signs and social
gestures that cannot be retrieved. More than any scholar in the
twentieth century, Joachim Jeremias attempted an "archaeology"
of the parables by restoring their Aramaic wording. His important
efforts notwithstanding, the recovery of an "original" parable has
proved impossible because the original once belonged to an acous-
tical rather than a textual moment, a singularity that will never again
exist. Socrates argued against books as useless tools, since they cannot expand or enlarge upon their arguments but only repeat the
same words over again. On very different grounds, Luther spoke of
the written Scripture as a fall from a more primal and kerygmatic
experience of orality. In the case of the parables, both men were
right—and wrong.

What is lost in writing can never be recovered. The written text
creates an unbridgeable distance between the reader and the original speaker, audience, and situation. What is gained in writing is a
new objectivity of the story that allows for greater freedom of interpretation. As Sandra Schneiders observes, cut off from its author's
intent, the text "begins to live its own life as a medium of meaning."
That we can no longer ask the original performer about his intention in telling the story means that the text now has the capacity
to address new audiences and unforeseen situations (Schneiders,
Revelatory Text, 142–44). The persistence of the text, long after the
spoken word has disappeared into thin air, creates the permanence
8   of a semantic witness as well as the possibility of new contexts of
meaning. Thanks to the written text, communities of every era may
"hear" the word of God.

The change in genre from speaking to writing presents one sort of difficulty, mainly for Bible specialists. But the most pervasive, if largely unarticulated, objection to the parables has to do with their form: they are narratives. In an era that has reduced wisdom to speedily delivered units of information, parables belong to the horse-and-buggy era of religious discourse. The prominence of narrative theology, ethics, and preaching that crested in the 1970s has been replaced by a bottom-line impatience with spiritual truths that cannot be delivered in sound bites, PowerPoints, rules, or religious "laws." As Fred Craddock said, it is as if a father might tell his child at bedtime, "Daddy is too busy to tell you the story of Little Red Riding Hood tonight. Let him tell you the *point* instead." Any narrative, even a short one, requires time for absorption, reflection, and implementation. The parable's tendency to dive for deeper truths appears radically unsuited to the contemporary surfing mentality.

The many problems we have associated with the parables, however, are accompanied by corresponding strengths. Yes, the parables are narratives, but they are short ones! As the great cultural critic Walter Benjamin announced in the 1930s, "Modern man no longer works at what cannot be abbreviated" (*Illuminations*, 93). To those who are susceptible to TV commercials and music videos, for whom "text" is a verb, to whom tweeting is the ultimate in self-expression, the parables have a certain cultural cache. Studies have repeatedly shown that the most successful commercials "tell a story." A commercial for an automobile or a skin conditioner that causes the viewer to reevaluate one's worth as a human being—all within the space of thirty seconds—bears the earmarks of a perversely effective parable.

What is true of the TV commercial is doubly true of the cell-phone novel gaining popularity in Japan and elsewhere. Cell-phone novels are written collaboratively by busy commuters who don't have time or space in their backpacks for *War and Peace*. If it is a good story, it must fit on the screen of a smart phone! This new breed of reader has not given up on narrative, but it has radically altered the definition and social function of "story." Thus the short stories of Jesus, many of which can be told in less than a minute, may honor the universal love of story as well as our culture's impatience with lengthy narratives.

Recently a popular magazine challenged its readers to state "The Gospel in Seven Words" (Heim). Of the twelve selections,

9

half were in narrative form, for example, "He led captivity captive," or "The wall of hostility has come down." Readers were delighted with the challenge of putting "the whole thing" in a rhetorical thimble. The submissions and the reader response to them made clear one overriding expectation: even the largest and wisest of truths must fit into a small space.

The French cultural critic François Lyotard decreed that the postmodern temper is marked by "incredulity toward all metanarratives" (*Postmodern Condition*, 67). He was referring to narratives that will *not* fit on the screen of a cell phone or into a seven-word sentence. Grand narratives offer a comprehensive account of the human condition from beginning to end. They explain everything. In virtue of their pervasive totality, they dominate the conscious and unconscious thinking of entire civilizations. Whether Marxist, capitalist, Freudian, religious, or scientific, these narratives impose their peculiar order on all thought and behavior. When thoroughly internalized, they are the filters that cause us to see the world in a particular way. Power relations of human origin, such as slavery, poverty, racial supremicism, the subjugation of women, homophobia, and even climate change—all are taken as "natural" to the way things were meant to be. As "totalizing" narratives, therefore, they often undergird oppression and inflict vast suffering on the world, whose victims can only narrate their counterstories in anguished response.

It seems clear that Jesus accepted the grand narrative of his own religious tradition, Palestinian Judaism. He lived and taught in constant reference to the key themes and demands of the Torah. He honored the law even as he disputed its significance vis-à-vis the continuing revelation of God's will. He framed his ministry in the mirror of the Scripture that formed him. He ended his brief life in observance of the feast of Passover. He acknowledged God's creation of the world and expected its future consummation. But Jesus also inspired a new and equally comprehensive narrative among those who worshiped him. His followers came to embrace his ministry, death, and resurrection as God's definitive story for the world, and he himself was hailed as Alpha and Omega, the beginning and end of all things. But Jesus told his grand narrative in piecemeal fashion, not as a story in which he was the supernatural hero, but in a series of insights, short stories, and episodic performances, all of which were geared to the lives of common people. Indeed, his parables function most effectively against the backdrop of larger

10

and more grandiose conceptions of God's rule. He compares the kingdom of God to a woman making bread. He reflects on the love of God amid the venal jealousies of family and village life. He likens the Almighty to a foolish father or a business agent looking for day laborers. A few of his parables he acts out. He uses a child as an object lesson for the kingdom of God and a poor widow as an illustration of true greatness.

One suspects that Jesus does not perform his stories for the sake of effective communication in clarifying a theological point, but offers them as a lens through which to glimpse the actual presence of the Divine in the ordinary situations he depicts. Thus his parables do not enshrine a body of truths but suggest a *method* of approaching and experiencing the truth. The implication of the parables is clear: if one cannot meet the kingdom of God amid the pots and pans of daily life, of what earthly use is the kingdom? It is precisely this scaled-back approach to his own grand narrative that appeals to those who today are turned off by the claims of religious institutions and the traditions of "Christendom."

Jesus had about forty stories in his repertoire (Hultgren, *Parables of Jesus*, 2–3, 3n6). How often he told them, with what degree of improvisation, and in exactly which contexts, we do not know. The Synoptic Gospels represent several traditions (*traditio* = the act of handing down), that is, processes of transmission that have now been permanently inscribed in written documents. The parables appear in separate versions and in a variety of settings. Occasionally variants of the same story appear to make different points, for example, the parable of the Lost Sheep (Matt. 18:10–14 and Luke 15:3–10) or the parable of the Great Feast (Matt. 22:1–14 and Luke 14:16–24). Some of Jesus' parables appear to have been augmented (and occasionally distorted) by later, editorial explanations (e.g., Mark 4:13–20 or Luke 16:9–13). In most cases it is impossible to identify a "first" telling from which the traditions, communities, writers, and editors fashioned their versions of the same story.

What we do know is that all the parables are built around exceedingly simple and vivid images: a little rich boy swilling hogs, a housewife tirelessly searching for a lost penny, a shepherd placing one of his beloved sheep on his shoulders, a hypocritical theologian at prayer, the humiliation of a guest who has worn the wrong dress at a fancy party. These images have stolen their way into our hearts. Their appeal in a visual culture cannot be overestimated.

11

Moreover, they are serious little stories—not entertainments or illustrations of other truths. If you allow yourself to take them seriously, they offer the unexpected possibility of loss or gain—your own experience of "outer darkness" versus the light and warmth of the father's house. Most of the parables present a world of zero-sum encounters in which halfway commitments or equivocal outcomes do not occur. They offer what one literary critic calls "the concrete universal"—the whole of life, including the life choices of the reader—all contained within the particularities of a singular narrative. One thinks of the ways in which Ernest Hemingway's *The Old Man and the Sea* or Harper Lee's *To Kill a Mockingbird* capture the largest possible meaning within the story of one character and a single act of courage.

Finally, the parables of Jesus undercut the grand narrative in another, often unnoticed way. They are secular stories in which God does not appear (the parable of the Rich Fool being an exception). The very absence of a visible character named "God" serves to level the playing field between the parables' hearers in the first century and us, the parables' readers in the twenty-first century. The parables originally spoke to a people who lived beneath a sacred canopy; today they address the default secularity of Western culture, a sad and impoverished landscape, yet one in which longing for glimpses of the supernatural cannot be suppressed. Now as then, the parables do not grant a beatific vision of God or a miraculous escape via the deus ex machina characteristic of classical theater. But even if God does not appear as a character in the parables, as he does, say, in the book of Job, the possibility of salvation does make itself known. The parables insist that we will meet God in the usual circumstances of time, space, and language, or we will not meet God at all. We will be saved at home, at work, or in the village, or we will not be saved at all. What Father Abraham says to the rich man in hell who longs for supernatural intervention, the parables say about the men and women of our generation: "'They have Moses and the prophets; they should listen to them'" (Luke 16:29).

No theologian took the secularity of the parables more seriously than Dietrich Bonhoeffer. In the letters he wrote from prison, he confessed that the familiar use of God language made him uneasy. He was offended by the chatter of religious people and their reliance upon the supernatural. He insisted that the "gaps" in knowledge and experience should not be filled by inspirational or

12

compensatory references to "God." For Bonhoeffer, the worldliness of the parables was not incidental to their character but essential to their saving power. It was *precisely* the apparent absence of the supernatural in Bonhoeffer's world (and in his own life) that lent him comfort in his distress. Paradoxically, it was God's absence that enkindled hope in a new way of acknowledging God's presence in the worst of situations: "It will be a new language," he wrote, "perhaps quite non-religious, but liberating and redeeming—as was Jesus' language" (*Letters and Papers*, 176–77, 300).

The Deep Source

We need parables because of two equally deep mysteries: the mystery of God and the mystery of human life. Yahweh introduces himself to Moses with the words "I AM WHO I AM" (Exod. 3:14). The metaphysical reality of this name, however, is hidden from Moses beneath the figure of a burning bush. Later at Sinai, Moses wants more than a symbolic manifestation, and so he says, "Show me your glory," but the Lord replies, "You cannot see my face; for no one shall see me and live." So God hides Moses in the cleft of the rock and covers him with his "hand" until his glory passes by (33:18–23). Moses cannot observe and therefore cannot describe the essence of God, which in Scripture is counted a mercy. No one can safely look directly at the sun or into a burning bush without protective lenses.

The same sense of mystery pervades human life. Who can "see" the design in the many contrarieties of joy and suffering, opportunity and failure, hope and despair that shape a single life or determine the fortunes of an entire family? Who can demonstrate exactly how God uses individuals, communities, or nations for a higher purpose? Even believers who acknowledge God's role in their lives may have difficulty distinguishing between grace and good luck. How then can anyone speak unambiguously or prosaically of God's presence in any human life? Biblical writers knew that the complexities of the divine-human relationship require a different sort of language, one that both honors the mystery from a distance and in fear and trembling attempts to penetrate it.

God shields us from close encounter with the mystery: Our cleft in the rock is the language of comparison. There are many

13

types of comparison, and later we shall examine them in greater detail. Parable is but one of them. The English word comes directly from the Greek *para-ballō*, "to cast beside." One entity or idea is "cast beside" another. A parable rubs the mystery of human life against the mystery of God in order to produce a new understanding of the two together, which is a revelation.

In the Septuagint (the ancient Greek translation of the Old Testament) the word "parable" is used to translate those figures of speech whose effectiveness relies on comparison. English has many words for these figures, such as analogy, metaphor, proverb, saying, byword, taunt, fable, riddle, and so forth; but Hebrew is largely restricted to one term: *māšāl*, plural *měšālîm* (*š* = *sh*; see Scott, *Hear the Parable*, 8–30; cf. Snodgrass, *Stories with Intent*, 7–11). *Māšāl* has a broad range of meanings, none of which precisely designates what modern interpreters call a parable. In the Old Testament *māšāl* can have one of three meanings: (1) to be like, (2) to represent, (3) to rule, in the sense that the *māšāl* creates a new power relation among individuals and groups. The prophets created *měšālîm* and launched them like missiles against Israel's enemies.

Essentially, a *māšāl* states or implies a comparison. The psalmist writes,

> Answer me quickly, O LORD;
> my spirit fails.
> Do not hide your face from me,
> or I shall be like [*m-š-l*] those who go down to the Pit.
> (Ps. 143:7)

The psalmist is saying, "Your silence, O God, is like death to me."

The many forms of *měšālîm* in the Old Testament illumine the rich sources of Jesus' poetic expressiveness. His use of them reflects the rhetorical universe he inhabited. Let me illustrate with a few examples:

Proverb. The proverb expresses a practical truth by means of sententious speech—sharp and barbed language marked by antithesis. Its ability to display both sides of the coin, as it were, in a few words makes the saying memorable. The speaker's command of the human condition, displayed in the crispness of delineating it, invests both the speaker and the saying with moral authority:

14

A soft answer turns away wrath,
    but a harsh word stirs up anger. (Prov. 15:1–2)
The wicked flee when no one pursues,
    but the righteous are as bold as a lion. (28:1)
All who exalt themselves will be humbled,
    but all who humble themselves will be exalted.
        (Jesus, in Matt. 23:12//Luke 14:11; 18:14)

Notice Jesus' use of chiasmus—the inversion of word order and grammatical structure in the sentence. The snappy *form* of this saying tells the hearer, "Listen and remember: this is important!" Jesus' pronouncement on humility is so versatile that it functions as a capstone to three different parables or parabolic acts (Luke 18:14; 14:14; Matt. 18:14). One thinks of Martin Luther King Jr.'s use of a similar form that he, too, employed in various situations of conflict:

If a man hasn't found something worth dying for,
    he isn't fit to live.

Taunt, derisive saying. The psalmist complains,

You have made us a byword [*māšāl*] among the nations,
    a laughingstock [a shaking of the head] among the peoples.
        (Ps. 44:14).

The prophet is instructed,

You will take up this taunt [*māšāl*]
    against the king of Babylon: . . .
"How you are fallen from heaven,
    O Day Star, son of Dawn!
How you are cut down to the ground,
    You who laid the nations low!"
        (Isa. 14:4, 12)

Jesus does not taunt his opponents, but he does deploy senttentious language in the heat of controversy. When his former neighbors take offense at him, Jesus says, "A prophet is not without honor except in his own country and in his own house," and he refuses to do a mighty work among them (Matt. 13:57 RSV). Against the scribes and Pharisees, he speaks a harsher word and, in case they miss his meaning, he supplements the metaphor with a clear explanation:

15

> For you are like whitewashed tombs,
> which on the outside look beautiful,
>> but inside they are full of the bones of the dead and all kinds of filth.
> So you also on the outside look righteous to others,
>> but inside you are full of hypocrisy and lawlessness.

(Matt. 23:27–28)

Riddle. What has four wheels and flies? What is red and smells like blue paint? How many graduate students does it take to change a lightbulb? Some riddles are fun, others may prove lethal. In Judges 14:14 Samson poses this riddle to the Philistines at Timnah:

> Out of the eater came something to eat,
>> Out of the strong came something sweet.

They solve it only after pressuring his wife to coax the meaning out of him; whereupon Samson replies with yet another *māšāl*:

> If you had not plowed with my heifer,
>> you would not have found out my riddle.

(v. 18b)

Matthew 22 presents a dangerous game of riddles. The Pharisees begin it by asking whether it is lawful or not to pay taxes to the emperor. The Sadducees continue the game with the riddle of the woman with seven dead husbands. A lawyer jumps in with the question of the greatest commandment (which in Luke 10:29 is followed by a trickier riddle, "But who is my neighbor?"). The chapter ends with Jesus posing his own riddle, "What do you think of the Messiah? Whose son is he?" (Matt. 22:42). The obvious answer, "the son of David," elicits another more perplexing riddle from Jesus:

> How is it then that David by the Spirit calls him Lord, saying,
>> "The Lord said to my Lord,
>>> 'Sit at my right hand,
>>> until I put your enemies under your feet'"?
> If David thus calls him Lord,
>> how can he be his son?

(vv. 43–46)

Game over! Earlier he had stumped the chief priests with the question "Did the baptism of John come from heaven, or was it of human origin?" (Matt. 21:25), to which there was no "right" answer.

16

Finally we hear echoes of the riddle form in Jesus' commentary on the healing of the paralytic: "Which is easier—to say to the paralytic, 'Your sins are forgiven,' or to say, 'Stand up and take your mat and walk'?" (Mark 2:9).

Most of Jesus' conversation partners cannot keep up with him. The desperate and audacious Syrophoenician woman is a notable exception (Mark 7:24–30 RSV): "Lord, yet even the dogs under the table eat the children's crumbs." Her example encourages us all to hang in there with this clever and authoritative teacher. His words are sharp, "piercing to the division of soul and spirit, . . . and discerning the thoughts and intentions of the heart" (Heb. 4:12 RSV); but to those who trust in God, the very same words offer healing, forgiveness, and peace.

The few allegories and parables found in the Old Testament we will reserve for our later discussion of the parables of Jesus. This brief sampling of his poetic diction, however, suggests two preliminary conclusions: It confirms our view of Jesus as one who spoke in the poetic tradition of the sages, singers, and liturgists of Israel. According to the evidence of the New Testament, Jesus rarely departed from the metaphoric register of comparison and reversal. Although the tradition offers ample evidence of Jesus as the eschatological prophet who created vivid scenarios of the new age, we cannot overlook the poetic side of Jesus usually associated with the practice of "wisdom." The interplay of these "two different mentalities," as Marcus Borg refers to them, remains the subject of ongoing debate (Borg, *Jesus in Scholarship*, 82–83).

The poetic character of Jesus' ministry suggests a new and revised view of the Christian preacher. Our managerial and technocratic age threatens to reduce the ministry to an exercise of organizational skills and technique; many sermons consist of a neat list of bullet-pointed conclusions projected on a screen, as if at a sales meeting. But if we really listen to Jesus, we cannot help but notice that the Christian message trades in pointed words of a different sort, vivid pictures, imaginative language, and a new view of everyday life from which God is not absent or relegated to the margins.

Jesus created his powerful images from the lumber room of Israel's Scripture, the depths of his own heart, and a keen shepherd's eye for the lost and straying. The preacher too has a vocation in these rhetorical and theological crafts. Like the language

17

of Jesus, the preaching of every generation draws on the ordinary moral and linguistic world of its listeners, employing what Fred B. Craddock refer to as "the nod of recognition." It then stretches recognition to the breaking point in order to present something new and unheard of, producing what Craddock (and Henry James) terms "the shock of recognition." In this, the preacher's work resembles that of a minor poet. T. S. Eliot declared that every culture needs its minor poets to balance the contributions of its major poets, who trade in the enormous myths that undergird civilization. Minor poets open small windows through which ordinary people may re-view their own stories against the light of the dominant myth. This is the work of parable and the task of the preacher, who, as Craig Barnes reminds us, belongs to the company of "minor poets" (*Pastor as Minor Poet*, 24–27; cf. Lischer, *End of Words*, 104).

Definition: Literary Effect

The best-known modern definition of a parable was given by C. H. Dodd in 1935: "At its simplest the parable is a metaphor or simile drawn from nature or common life, arresting the hearer by its vividness or strangeness, and leaving the mind in sufficient doubt about its precise application to tease it into active thought" (*Parables of the Kingdom*, 5; Donahue, *Gospel in Parable*, 5–20, on Dodd). There is little to add to Dodd's excellent definition except two observations. First, Dodd's definition omits the single most distinctive characteristic of Jesus' parables: they are narratives. In focusing on metaphor and simile, Dodd neglects to mention that in a parable these two figures of speech generate brief narrative extensions, which by definition include the following elements: plot, setting, conflict, character types, denouement, and point of view. A narrative offers something greater than a stunning or perplexing figure of speech. It has a beginning, a middle, and an end. A narrative provides a vehicle for the listener's identification with the action or characters in the story.

The parables exist on several narrative continua: from magic to realism, from tragedy to comedy, from the social world to the personal, and from hostile audiences to friendly ones. Listeners

18

may locate themselves at various points on the narrative spectrum: Some of us are lost, some are found, and some have only begun the journey home. Some of us are delighted by these little stories, some are puzzled, some are offended by them, and all three responses often coexist in the same hearer. The parables of Jesus also establish genetic links between a series of smallish narratives and the evangelists' larger story of Jesus' life and ministry. We shall return to these observations later in the chapter.

The second observation is more positive than the first. Dodd's definition has the virtue of describing what parables *do* in the sensibilities of the listener. In Dodd's forty-one-word definition of a parable, twenty-five of his words, or approximately 61 percent, deal with the *effect* of a parable on its hearer. Whatever we conclude about the history, form, and content of Jesus' parables, everyone agrees that he was trying to *do* something by telling them. In Klyne Snodgrass's phrase, they are "stories with intent" or, in the word of the philosopher J. L. Austin, they are "illocutionary," or performative utterances (Snodgrass, *Stories with Intent*, 17; Austin, *How to Do Things with Words*).

For example, it is possible to speak a simple narrative sentence, "The game is over," in at least two distinct registers. One is purely descriptive of the state of play; the second is heavy with finality, spoken by someone with the authority to end the game. The parables of Jesus operate in both registers. First, by their realistic evocation of village life and human behavior, they create a model of the still-recognizable world. Second, by means of the shock produced by some deeper realization, they engage the reader on a very different intellectual and emotional level. They never impose their will in a heavy-handed manner, but merely invite the unsuspecting listener into a harmless little story in which something odd and possibly disorienting will occur. When Dodd uses words like "arresting," "strangeness," "doubt," and especially the verb "tease," he is evoking with near-clinical precision the flurry of suspicion, confusion, delight, and insight at work in the acoustical-sensory apparatus as it receives an incoming parable. The mind's reaction to the metaphor goes something like this: "No way! → How can that be? → It's true!" The paradoxical *is / is not* reaction, which has been analyzed in many studies of metaphor, represents a cognitive experience that occurs with lightning-like speed. When the process is slowed down, 19 picked apart, and explained, as scholars and critics are apt to do, the metaphor, like a good joke, is ruined.

Definition: Kingdom of God

Dodd's definition of parable is strictly formal and literary. It has nothing to say about its religious substance, which is perplexing, since it was Dodd who among twentieth-century scholars focused most decisively on the kingdom of God as the referent of Jesus' parables. A second definition is therefore needed to supplement Dodd's formalistic approach. Bernard Brandon Scott defines the parable in reference to three criteria: literary form, social location, and theological reference. Thus a parable is "a *māšāl* that employs a short narrative fiction to reference a transcendent symbol" (*Hear the Parable*, 8). We have already discussed the importance of *māšāl* and narrative in the parables of Jesus. But what is the "symbol" to which they bear witness? Most of the parables either explicitly or implicitly reference the kingdom of God, or in Matthew's circumlocution, "the kingdom of heaven." They ask, "With what can we compare the kingdom of God, or what parable will we use for it?" (Mark 4:30). Even parables that do not explicitly reference the kingdom, like the Pharisee and the Tax Collector, or the Good Samaritan, are widely considered to be narrative illustrations of life in the kingdom of God.

Jesus began his ministry by announcing the tangible nearness of the reign of God. Israel had always acknowledged Yahweh's sovereignty in the person of Israel's king and in the majesty of the created order, which in its own idiom declares the glory of God. Yahweh's kingship was celebrated annually in the enthronement of God's stand-in, the king of Israel.

> I will tell of the decree of the LORD:
> He said to me, "You are my son;
>   today I have begotten you."
>   (Ps. 2:7)

The same Lord "breaks the cedars" and "shakes the wilderness. . . . The Lord sits enthroned over the flood [firmament]; the Lord sits enthroned as king forever" (Ps. 29, esp. vv. 5, 8, 10).

20

Psalm 97 introduces another—ethical—strand of Israel's celebration of God's reign when it proclaims,

> Righteousness and justice are the foundation of his throne. . . .
> The LORD loves those who hate evil;
> he regards the lives of his faithful;
> he rescues them from the hand of the wicked."
> (97:2b, 10)

The proclamation of God's justice rests upon a single act, the deliverance of Israel from captivity. The same God who created the
natural order also created a people and delivered them from bondage in Egypt. God is the king whose reign bridges the world of
nature, with all its beauty and fury, and the world of human history,
marred by suffering and injustice. Psalm 136 unites the two spheres
of God's reign by means of a refrain repeated twenty-six times, "For
his steadfast love endures forever" (Norman Perrin, *Jesus and the
Language of the Kingdom*, 16–20).

When he began his ministry, Jesus reframed the proclamation
of God's rule in three ways:

1. He toured Galilee, "teaching in their synagogues and proclaiming the good news of the kingdom" (Matt. 4:23). By doing so
he reinvented the notion of "kingdom," or "reign," for he preached
to a colonized people who had not known a real king in Israel for a
long time. The only reign known to them was the tyranny of Rome
and its surrogates.

2. He spoke of the kingdom as an eruption *in* history rather
than outside it or at its end. "The time is fulfilled," he says in Mark
1:15, "and the kingdom of God has come near." He later speaks of
the kingdom as a reality *with* a history of its own and outlines its
chronological stages culminating in the death of John the Baptist.

3. Finally, he personalized the kingdom in his own ministry of
justice and righteousness. His mission to the poor, blind, lame, and
oppressed of Galilee signaled the return of God's dynamic authority
in Israel. At Nazareth, after reading Isaiah's vision of the messianic
kingdom, he concludes with a rabbinic gloss that surprises and out-
rages his former neighbors: "*Today* this scripture has been fulfilled
in your hearing" (Luke 4:21, emphasis added).

The conceptualization of "the kingdom of God" by biblical
scholars and theologians has obscured the surge of excitement

21

that must have been produced by Jesus' message, for what he proclaimed was not a concept but a dawning reality. His entire ministry reaffirmed a faith that Israel had long held but was in danger of forgetting: "God still rules! God will heal you of your infirmities, forgive your sins, and set you free from every form of oppression. Get ready! Those with ears to hear, let them hear." But the reign of God will not come in cosmic signs to be observed, so that one might say, "'Lo, here it is!' or 'There!' for behold, the kingdom of God is in the midst of you" (Luke 17:21 RSV).

The hiddenness of the kingdom is exemplified by the tiny parable in Matthew 13:33 (Luke 13:20–21), in which a woman *"hid"* (RSV; not "mixed in," as in NRSV) a pinch of yeast in three measures of flour. Although leaven frequently carries negative connotations (e.g., Matt. 16:6; 1 Cor. 5:6–8; Gal. 5:9), this is a story of a woman making bread, and for that yeast is essential. The pinch of yeast will leaven three measures of flour, enough flour to produce between sixty and eighty loaves of bread (Hultgren, 406–7). The kingdom is on the rise, and its agent is not a holy man in the temple but a woman in her kitchen.

Later, when the Pharisees ask for the details of the kingdom's arrival (Luke 17:20), the conversation turns away from seeds or a hidden pinch of yeast to something larger and more spectacular. To his disciples, Jesus gives an answer that initially appears to contradict his admonition against "things that can be observed," for it predicts the pyrotechnic return of the Son of Man, a mysterious figure of whom Jesus consistently speaks in the third person. Indeed, the word "kingdom" drops out of his response to their question in Luke 17, and the Son of Man moves center stage. But before the Son of Man appears in glory, "he" (the Son of Man—but in this context, Jesus?) will continue to subsist amid the ordinary sufferings, persecutions, and uncertainties of this life. When the Son of Man makes himself known, however, those who live in expectation must not hesitate or consider other options. "Remember Lot's wife" (Luke 17:32), Jesus says laconically.

Mark and Matthew paint even more developed apocalyptic scenarios, neither of which explicitly joins the "kingdom of God" to the end times or the dramatic appearance of the Son of Man (Mark 13//Matt. 24). In a shared tradition in which "kingdom of God" and "Son of Man" are not associated with each other, several identical themes and narrative tendencies appear. In both Gospels the scene shifts from local observations of temple architecture ("What large stones and what large buildings!"), to intimations of global warfare, followed by predictions of cosmic tribulation. The mention of persecution and betrayal clearly predicts (or reflects) the experience of the church after Jesus' ascension. Like many apocalyptic scenarios, a futurist view of the kingdom serves as a present source of confirmation for the beleaguered followers of Jesus. The cosmic references comfort the Jesus people with visions of their Lord's universal sovereignty. As vivid as these scenarios are, however, Jesus strictly forbids the church from losing its bearings by engaging in fanciful predictions and senseless arguments about the date of his reappearing.

The absence of kingdom talk in this material has led some scholars to dissociate the kingdom of God from an apocalyptic climax at the end of time (e.g., Borg, *Jesus in Scholarship*, 7). And yet, some sort of future reckoning is inscribed throughout the Gospels and in selected parables as well, so much so as to place a heavy burden of proof on those who would separate the message of the kingdom from a cosmic revelation at the end. The later parables of the Thief in the Night, the Wise Slave, the Foolish and Wise Virgins, and the Talents—all rely on a final reckoning for their narratives to make sense (cf. Matt. 24:43–51; 25:1–30). Even the optimistic seed parables of the kingdom, clustered at the beginning of Jesus' ministry, point toward a consummation at the end. When the grain is ripe, Jesus says, the farmer "goes in with his sickle, because the harvest has come" (Mark 4:29).

In Matthew 13:24–30 Jesus compares the kingdom of heaven to a wheat field in which an enemy has sown weeds. The servants have a mind to separate the good from the bad immediately, but the owner instructs them to let the plants grow together until the harvest, when the weeds will be gathered into bundles and burned. In his allegorical explanation of the parable (vv. 36–43), Jesus explicitly integrates the Son of Man and the kingdom in one story and reserves divine justice for the final conflagration.

The question, then, is not, Did Jesus (or the church after him) fuse the Son of Man and the kingdom of God? He (or the tradition) clearly did so. The question is, Who is the Son of Man? If it is Jesus, why does he not say "I"? What is it about his earthly circumstances and identity that separates him from the heavenly-like figure portrayed in the book of Daniel, to whom universal dominion is given? "His dominion is an everlasting dominion that shall not

23

pass away, and his kingship is one that shall never be destroyed" (Dan. 7:14b). If the notation "Son of Man" represents the church's post-resurrection interpretation of his majesty, what was its motive in failing to clarify the relationship of Jesus to this supernatural figure? Or, if the parable is original to Jesus and the allegorical explanation in Matthew 13:36–43 is the work of a later community, as many scholars believe, why doesn't the allegory at least identify Jesus with the Son of Man? Why not come out with it and acknowledge that it is none other than Jesus of Nazareth who sows good seed (v. 37), and the very same Jesus who will send his angels in final judgment (v. 41)?

One must remember that the absence of "I" language on the lips of Jesus is not limited to passages in which the Son of Man plays an apocalyptic role: "the Son of Man [that is, "I, Jesus"] came eating and drinking" (Matt. 11:19a); "The Son of Man is going as it has been determined, but woe to that one by whom he is betrayed (Luke 22:22; cf. also Matt. 20:28//Mark 10:45). One must also remember the many occasions on which Jesus instructs his disciples to keep quiet about his identity and miracles. More than a century's worth of critical thinking has not solved the problem of Jesus' relation to the Son of Man. Absent a compelling theory, however, we have sufficient evidence in the parables themselves (see above) to link the kingdom to a future consummation and Jesus to the Son of Man.

The discussion of the kingdom of God often veers into territory marked by concepts, dates, and data. The more specific the data, the more cramped and overcoded is the concept. If the kingdom refers only to a set of occurrences that will take place at a specified time, the power of God in daily life is effectively minimized. The history of Christianity is littered with predictions of Jesus' return and blueprints for his future reign. However, they do not begin from a theology of God's abiding presence but from an overweening confidence in the interpreter's mastery of the data. One thinks of the American Millerites, who calculated the Lord's return based on the numbers given in the book of Daniel. On October 22, 1844, they abandoned their jobs and headed for the high ground to greet the returning Lord. It was a long night, now commemorated in American religious lore as "the Great Disappointment."

Scholarly discussion of the kingdom has shifted from "concept" to "symbol," for if we have learned anything from Jesus' use of the term "reign of God," it is that its referent cannot be specified by date or equated with a political or social movement (Norman Perrin, *Jesus and the Language of the Kingdom*, 33–34). A symbol is less determinate, more open-ended, and more creative than a concept. A genuine symbol, like the word "cross" or a physical crucifix, does not merely point to the thing it represents but mysteriously actualizes the power of the symbol and makes it present.

Bernard Brandon Scott describes a symbol as a "nebula" of meanings swirling around a concept (*Hear the Parable*, 58). This is an attractive way of relating to a symbol and in many ways captures the multivalence of the Bible's use of "the kingdom of God." The notion of "king" has long been perceived as a problem in modern usage. The preacher and social prophet Clarence Jordan regularly translated "kingdom of God" with "the God Movement," thereby eliminating both monarchical and gender-based objections. What is lost in his translation is the connotation of authority in the word "rule." In Jesus' day, kings actually ruled. In contemporary usage the terms "kingdom" or "reign" may have greater, not less, metaphorical stretch than in their biblical usage: they evoke structural and interpersonal relations of authority not limited to actual kings or visible rulers. And the word "God" covers every conceivable meaning, from the Oblong Blur of the deists to the specifications and attributes of the world's many religions. Thus on closer inspection, the image of a *nebula* doesn't help much in symbolizing the kingdom of God. True, the parables of Jesus are less precise than a concept, but they offer more than a nebula of meanings. The parables qualify the traditional notions of both "reign" and "God" in particular ways. They help us comprehend the kingdom, much in the way the rabbis said that the proverbs of Solomon—his "parables"—provided "handles" for the Torah, thereby enabling readers to grasp its meaning. By analogy to the rabbinic saying, Scott suggests that the parables of Jesus are our "handles" on the kingdom of God (*Hear the Parable*, 52–53, 61–62) Instead of reconceptualizing the phrase, Jesus allows us to take hold of its referent, the dynamic but hidden authority of God. With disarming simplicity he performs the kingdom, as if to say, "My father (your Lord) makes his claim on you in the following unexpected manner: '*There was a man who had two sons. . . .*'"

25

Perhaps a parable will help us understand the mystery of Jesus' parables: While seeking the fabled wisdom of the Kingdom of

Parable, a teacher and her students fell into a deep ditch of misunderstanding. Professor Reason and Reverend Religion understood the depth of the problem but were unable or unwilling to help. They passed by on the other side. Finally a poor vagabond dressed in less than regal manner, with tattered jeans and a hole in his boots, stopped and pulled them out of the ditch. Who was this unassuming savior? To their astonishment, the teacher and her students had been rescued by the very one they had set out to master. Those with ears to hear, . . .

The debate over the timing of the kingdom has obscured another of its more important characteristics. The kingdom is an event. When it dawns, it precipitates a response among those who are confronted by it: It produces a crisis (Greek *krisis* = judgment). Many of the parables of Jesus begin with a crisis and proceed either to deliverance or to utter loss (Via, *The Parables*, 101). For example, when we first meet the Dishonest Steward, he has just been called into the boss's office for an inspection of his books (Luke 16). The story begins in an air of managed panic. The parable we know as the Good Samaritan begins with a mugging and a robbery (Luke 10). The story of the Weeds among the Wheat begins with a senseless act of vandalism (Matt. 13).

A crisis can occur at any moment in life—or at its end. In medicine, the crisis moment is the turning point at which the patient will either improve or die. A crisis presents us with the proverbial "dangerous opportunity." To his great credit, C. H. Dodd understood that the crisis Jesus provoked was not limited to the end times or the last judgment; rather, he located it at the heart of Jesus' earthly ministry of preaching and healing, which means that the church of every era, including our own, is addressed by the demands of the kingdom. Dodd has been justly criticized for underestimating the future dimension of God's rule, but it was Dodd who definitively joined the parables of Jesus to the kingdom of God. If Adolf Jülicher discovered many points among the parables, Dodd found the one thing needful. The title of his book says it all: *The Parables of the Kingdom*.

Dodd coined the phrase "realized eschatology" to describe the judgment that erupts ahead of time, as it were, whenever and wherever human beings are confronted by the claims of Jesus. To make his point, Dodd relied on passages such as Mark 1:15: "The time is fulfilled, and the kingdom of God has come near"; Matthew 12:28: "But if it is by the Spirit of God that I cast out demons, then the

26

kingdom of God has come to you" ("upon you" RSV; Luke 10:9b: "Say to them, 'The kingdom of God has come near to you'"; and Luke 17:21: "The kingdom of God is in the midst of you" (RSV). Realized eschatology puts the stress back where it belongs: on us and our response to the Lord's advent in our lives. The parables function as signal flares calling attention to the dangerous opportunities presented by the reign of God in our world. They are coded messages that activate the secrets of the kingdom. They *are* the kingdom breaking into speech. Because to some degree the kingdom is *realized*, that is, present among us, the parables will continue to be performed as long as there are hearers with ears to hear.

Rabbis, Judaism, and the "Originality" of Jesus

The Old Testament contains few parables of the sort that Jesus told. One immediately thinks of the story of the ewe lamb with which Nathan snares King David (2 Sam. 12) as well as several others, including Jotham's fable of the trees (Judg. 9), Isaiah's Song of the Vineyard in 5:1–7, his Parable of the Farmers in 28:23–29, and the Parody of the Idol in 40:18–20 (for others, see 2 Sam. 14:4–17; 1 Kings 20:39–42). The prophet Ezekiel, too, is rich in allegorical and parabolic language. These relatively isolated examples, however, do not allow us to trace Jesus' narratives back to his Scriptures.

Likewise, from Jesus' contemporaries, notably the Pharisees, we hear no parables like those found in the New Testament—no masters and servants, lost sheep or coins, leaven, seeds, weeds, or treasure in a field; no prodigal sons, dishonest stewards, unforgiving servants, or wrathful kings. Little in the way of parable production can be documented from Jesus' religious context or the two to three generations that followed it. The sayings of the rabbis collected in the Mishnah (from the Hebrew *šānāh*, "to repeat," 200 CE) contains only one parable. Two scholars of the early Tannaim have concluded, "One may thus speak with confidence of the existence of rabbinic parables by the end of the first century CE, but not much earlier" (McArthur and Johnston, *Rabbinic Parables*, 165–66; cf. Bultmann, *The Synoptic Tradition*, 106–8). The forty parables of Jesus, then, stand alone at the headwaters of the great flow of rabbinic storytelling that appears about seventy-five years

27

after him and crests much later with the Amoraic rabbis in the high period of classical Rabbinic Judaism, in the third to the sixth centuries of the Common Era (Scott, *Hear the Parable*, 14–15, 17; cf. Snodgrass, *Stories with Intent*, 53–59).

Yet it is misleading to speak of the "originality" of Jesus as a storyteller, for such a comment appears to distance Jesus from the broad tradition of imaginative language that nurtured him and from which he drew sustenance his whole life. The Jewish scholar David Stern rejects "the glorification of Jesus' parables at the expense of the Rabbis'. Where Jesus' parables are typically described as vivid and lifelike, 'fresh as the air of the Galilean mountains,' in the words of Adolph Jülicher, . . . the Rabbinic parables have been characterized as pedantic, forced, and artificial, laden with the sullen dust of the classroom" (Stern, "Jesus' Parables," 42).

Although Christianity grew out of Judaism, and Judaism, as John Paul II declared, is "intrinsic" to Christianity, the two are more frequently understood by their differences than by the elements they hold in common (John Paul, quoted in Bockmuehl, "God's Life as a Jew," 76). A Jewish scholar has observed that polarization as a method of clarification leads to oversimplification, and this applies to the entire set of Jewish-Christian relations, including the study of parables (Flusser, "A New Sensitivity," 107). Current scholarship attempts to correct this misperception and to narrow the distance between Jesus the rabbi and Jesus the founder of the Christian movement. A good place to begin is by attending to the relationship of Jesus to the parabolic tradition of Judaism. Although rabbinic parables were preserved at a date later than New Testament parables, it is thought that the rudiments of parabolic style predated Jesus and contributed to what several scholars refer to as an early culture of Jewish parable. It is possible to hypothesize a broad and common source of parabolic discourse, out of which Jesus and the rabbis formed separate but related branches, and it is possible to do so without compromising what David Flusser terms Jesus' "unique and incomparable" understanding of God ("A New Sensitivity," 126; Thoma, "Rabbinic Parables"; Stern, "Jesus' Parables"; for a summary of the discussion, see Schottroff's comments on the work of Flusser and Stern in *Parables of Jesus*, 95; and Oldenhage, *Parables for Our Time*, 48–50).

28

We may learn a great deal about the distinctiveness of Jesus' stories by comparing them with those of the rabbis who succeeded him. Structurally, the rabbinic parables bear a family resemblance to the parables of Jesus. Rabbinic parables are brief narratives and often introduced with a question of comparison: "Unto what is the matter like?" The story is usually followed by a brief explanation or interpretation, the *nimšal*, which is introduced by "even so," "so," or "thus." The meaning often turns on what a rabbinic scholar identifies as "one meaningful moment," a glance, an aside, or a brief episode, the significance of which points well beyond itself. We see this technique reproduced in modern literature, not so much in parables as in short stories by such master storytellers as Edgar Allen Poe and Henry James (Thoma, "Rabbinic Parables," 31).

One major difference between Jesus and the rabbis lies in their field of concern. Where Jesus' stories reference the reign of God and almost never mention a biblical text (the parables of the Good Samaritan and the Wicked Tenants being exceptions), many rabbinic parables function exegetically to explain a particular passage of Scripture. They begin with a quotation from the passage in question, illuminate it by a simple comparison or story, and conclude with the repetition of the passage. Let one example suffice. Although its point is the reverse of Matthew 20:1–16, the Workers in the Vineyard, the dramatic setting and cast of characters (king, laborers) in the following rabbinic parable remind us of the "stock" characteristics of oral performances across the ancient world:

The Exceptional Laborer. "And I will have regard for you" (Lev. 26:9). They parable [tell] a parable. Unto what is the matter like? It is like a king who hired many laborers. And along with them was one laborer that had worked for him many days. All the laborers went to receive their pay for the day, and this one special laborer went also. He said to this one special laborer: I will have regard for you. The others, who have worked for me only a little, to them I will give small pay. You, however, will receive a large recompense.

Even so both the Israelites and the peoples of the world sought their pay from God. And God said to the Israelites: My children, I will have regard for you. The peoples of the world have accomplished very little for Me, and I will give them but a small reward. You, however, will receive a large recompense. Therefore it says: "And I will have regard for you."

(in McArthur and Johnston, *Rabbinic Parables*, 58)

29

Some have contrasted the mission of Jesus and the gift of the rabbis with the words "eschatological" and "exegetical," respectively (McArthur and Johnston, *Rabbinic Parables*, 172). The assessment is provisionally helpful since many of Jesus' parables are concerned with the relationship of contemporary behavior to the future of the kingdom—always in the shadow of the ministry and fate of their teller—while the majority of rabbinic parables draw from the history of Israel and Israel's unique mission in the world.

An additional stylistic difference demands our attention. In Christian circles it has become popular to dwell on the element of surprise or the reversal of expectations found in many of the parables of Jesus. This literary quality is sometimes claimed as a characteristic of *all* parables. In their study of rabbinic parables, Harvey McArthur and Robert Johnston remind us that Jesus was a "dissenter" and a "protester" vis-à-vis his inherited tradition, which would have necessarily lent to his narrative art the confounding element of reversal. But centuries of rabbinic storytelling teach us that parables are in it for the long haul: they provide longitudinal instruction in the art of faithful living. The authors conclude, "A parable is a parable whether it opens up a brand-new world for the listener or whether it simply illustrates, clarifies, or adorns a world long known" (*Rabbinic Parables*, 173–74; Snodgrass, *Stories with Intent*, 18–19). Given the presence of reversal in *most* of Jesus' parables, we might claim the epiphany associated with reversal—the *aha* experience—as the distinctive mark of *Jesus'* parables within the larger and diverse parabolic tradition.

These distinctions notwithstanding, Jesus clearly belongs to the rabbinic tradition of storytelling and teaching. The rabbi instructed his disciples on theological and practical matters of ultimate significance and, not unlike Jesus, sought to relate the wisdom of God and Torah to the ordinary affairs of life. Amid his circle of followers, the rabbi's mastery of truth, like that of the Lord, who taught "as one having authority" (Mark 1:22), was beyond dispute. The rabbi's students marveled at his wisdom, which he transmitted via clever analogies and vivid examples drawn from life, then sharpened and completed with oracular insight. As in the Jesus tradition, those who gathered around the teacher carefully filed his stories and pronouncements in memory, debated their meaning endlessly, and repeated them for the instruction and edification of future generations.

30

Types of Parables

The parables of Jesus have been classified according to three criteria: (1) the theological content of their message, (2) their literary
form, and (3) their social setting. Since these and other categories
will play a later role in our reading of the parables, we will briefly
summarize them here.

But before we do, let me point out the shortcomings of tax-
onomies in general. Classifications are always riddled by exceptions
and overlap; they are never absolute, and in the case of the parables
they never deliver quite as much as they promise. Still, in the New
Testament the parables do fall into groups arranged according to
theme and imagery, and their classification may provide a modest
set of "handles" for the interpreter.

Theological Content

The most thorough classification of the parables' theological
themes is found in Joachim Jeremias's *The Parables of Jesus*. He
was reacting to Jülicher's tendency to attach a generic moral to
each of Jesus' parables. Jülicher was, in turn, reacting against the
church's long practice of assigning to every detail of the parables
an allegorical meaning drawn from Christian doctrine or tradition. Jeremias was not only committed to a rigorously historical
investigation of the text and its transmission; he was also shaped by
his Lutheran understanding of salvation history. He knew that the
parables belonged to the historical Jesus, his immediate followers,
and to the next generation of the primitive church. As the foremost
archaeologist of the parables, Jeremias exposed several layers of
the parables' audience, which included Jesus' original hearers as
well as the church that came later. He convincingly demonstrated
that parables spoken against Jesus' opponents in the heat of the
moment underwent a radical transformation at the hands of the
evangelists and their Christian sources. Obscure metaphors were
exchanged for the certainties of allegorical teaching and example
stories; parables of provocation became teaching tools for the
church; present-tense crises were projected onto the screen of
future expectations. In the church's understanding of the parables,
Jesus became the subject matter of virtually all his own stories (Jeremias, *Parables of Jesus*, 33–89).

31

According to Jeremias, Jülicher was right to find only one meaning in each parable; he simply failed to discover the right one—the theological meaning. He failed to understand how deeply embedded Jesus' message was in the Judaism of his day, and how profoundly Christian and ecclesial the parables eventually became. To Jeremias, the parables yielded a thematic outline of salvation history, which he proceeded to expound in a series of chapters with such titles as "Now Is the Day of Salvation," "God's Mercy for Sinners," "The Great Assurance," "The Imminence of Catastrophe," "The Challenge of the Hour," and several other categories. On closer inspection, however, Jeremias's categories do not do justice to the complexities of many of the parables. For example, most of the parables in the category of "God's Mercy for Sinners" also heap God's judgment and wrath on those who do not respond to mercy. And other "mercy parables," such as the Pharisee and the Tax Collector, give collateral instruction on prayer and would fit neatly in another category. The Good Samaritan is included in the chapter on "Realized Discipleship," but the surprise heroics of a foreigner and its implied critique of the religious establishment make it a good candidate for several other categories. One could multiply the exceptions many times over (for another scheme, cf. Hultgren, *Parables of Jesus*, vii–ix, 2–5).

Others have approached the classification of the parables with a broader brush. Robert Capon, for example, speaks of parables of judgment, parables of grace, and parables of the kingdom, but the same objections apply even to his less complicated categories (*Parables of Grace*). Thus the story of the Workers in the Vineyard (Matt. 20:1–16), which Jeremias puts into the Mercy column, Capon relegates to Judgment. And the Good Samaritan, which Jeremias and others see as a role model for the Christian life, Capon assigns to Unmerited Grace. My point is not that Capon and Jeremias are wrong; in fact, Capon offers a helpful alternative to the usual atomization of the sayings and parables of Jesus: He interprets the parables by the light of Jesus' ministry, death, and resurrection, which joins Jesus' words and deeds and allows them to be read as a single story. But the elaborate classifications themselves— the "handles," as it were, which are common to virtually every book on the parables of Jesus—are so easily manipulated that they prove less than helpful to the average interpreter.

32

Literary Form: "True" Parable

Just as the Hebrew *māšāl* became the catchword for a variety of figures of speech, "parable" often designates any and all the stories Jesus told. Going back to Jülicher, and more recently, Dan O. Via, the basic distinction has been made between stories that contain an indirect or metaphoric element and those that do not. What is sometimes called a "true parable" is a freely invented short story with two or more characters whose action is cast into the past tense (on the forms, see Via, *The Parables*, 2–13). Moreover, it usually features an objective to be achieved; a complication, interference, or conflict; and an unexpected resolution, in which the objective is either gained or irrevocably missed. In a true parable, character is often exposed by means of dialogue, interior monologue, or soliloquy. For example, when the Prodigal says to himself, "How many of my father's hired hands have bread enough and to spare, but here I am dying of hunger!" his interior monologue helps propel the action toward its climax (Luke 15:17). True parable does not achieve its meaning by forging correlations with nature, doctrine, church, the history of Israel, or other obvious "markers," all of which lie outside the narrative itself. To the contrary, as C. H. Dodd said, its indefinite relation to such factors leaves the mind in sufficient doubt as to tease it into active thought. Thus the stories of the Weeds among the Wheat (minus its explanation by Jesus), the Prodigal Son, or the Unjust Judge, to name but a few, are true narrative parables: they satisfy most of the criteria listed above.

True parables are "extended metaphors" because their plots emerge from puzzling and sometimes perverse combinations of images or situations and ideas. Like a metaphor, something about these stories is either twisted or surprising. The image, or what the literary critic I. A. Richards termed the "vehicle," seems an odd companion for the religious idea, or "tenor," which the story is meant to evoke (*Philosophy of Rhetoric*, 96–100). In true parable, the tenor *borrows* the attributes of the vehicle, and the vehicle is imbued with the more abstract attributes of the tenor. "The reign of God" borrows its visualization from a man casting seeds in every direction—an unlikely combination, since kingly authority and sowing seeds have little to do with each other—and suddenly a homely agricultural activity is freighted with the suggestion of a

33

holy truth. The vehicle is transferred to or "moves upon" the tenor, and together they create something new. (In modern Greece a variant of *metaphorein* appears on the exterior of moving trucks!) The theological idea is greater than its picture, but it is lifeless without it. The tenor does not equal "the meaning" of the story, but meaning emerges from the interaction of tenor and vehicle.

The second major category of parables operates in a very different way. These are stories in which the element of indirection is muted or absent altogether; they are divided into three subgenres: (1) similitudes, (2) example stories, and (3) allegories.

1. The *similitude*, or "simple" parable, originates in the simile, a comparison that traditionally employs the word "like" or "as." Jesus used many similes, such as his warning to Peter, "Satan has demanded to sift you like wheat" (Luke 22:31); or his rebuke of the Pharisees, "For you [in your hypocrisy] are like whitewashed tombs." Then, to make sure they (and the wider audience) do not miss his point of comparison, he continues by explicating the simile, "which on the outside look beautiful, but inside they are full of the bones of the dead and of all kinds of filth. So you also on the outside look righteous to others, but inside you are full of hypocrisy and lawlessness" (Matt. 23:27–28). Thus the simile comes equipped with its own coordinates and therefore offers structural, built-in guidance to those seeking its meaning.

The similitude is a narrative simile. It is usually cast in the present tense and depicts a recurring, everyday activity, as here:

> The kingdom of God is as if someone should scatter seed on the ground, and would sleep and rise night and day, and the seed would sprout and grow, he does not know how. The earth produces of itself, first the stalk, then the head, then the full grain in the head. But when the grain is ripe, at once he goes in with his sickle because the harvest has come.
>
> (Mark 4:26–32)

It is true that the use of present or aorist subjunctive tense associates God's rule with the inevitability of the recurring cycles of agriculture and ordinary life; but it is also true that in Matthew 13, for example, some of these same activities are cast in the past tense as stories (e.g., vv. 33, 45).

We are also obliged to question the grade-school distinction between simile and metaphor based on the sole criterion of "like" or "as" in the sentence. Similes are not always predictable or easy to explicate, and metaphors do not always shock or exhilarate. Some metaphors are very tired and belong to what George Orwell in "Politics and the English Language" called "a huge dump of worn-out metaphors." For example, Flannery O'Connor concludes one of her greatest short stories, "A Temple of the Holy Ghost," with an unforgettable image, and one that illustrates my point. It occurs in the context of a little girl's discovery of the ways in which the cruelty of human beings coexists with the grace of God in a small southern town. At the end of the story the narrator reports, "The sun was a huge red ball like an elevated host drenched in blood." Notice that the so-called metaphor in this sentence is pedestrian at best (the sun = a red ball), but the simile, that part of speech that grammarians tell us is predictable and inferior to metaphor (the sun = *like* an elevated host drenched in blood), packs the real wallop in the sentence and teases out a powerful meaning from the story.

2. The *example story* lacks the symbolic or indirect element. Its theme appears to be an uncomplicated "Do this, Do not do that. Go and do likewise." The story of the Good Samaritan is usually considered a narrative example of how we, the hearers, ought to behave when confronted with the needs of others: we ought to follow the example of the Good Samaritan and help the unfortunate (Luke 10). Likewise, the parable of the Pharisee and the Tax Collector is often taken to be an example of how we ought to pray: not in pride like the Pharisee, but with the abject humility of the tax collector (Luke 18).

By the very nature of an example, this subgenre tends to be open-ended and lends itself to creative applications. The lesson of the Good Samaritan, for example, has been applied to every conceivable social issue ranging from race relations to abortion to capital punishment. Even in the most straightforward of examples, however, Jesus manages to throw a theological curve: in one parable, the hero is a despised foreigner and not the pious Jewish layperson Jesus' religious hearers likely expected; in another, the model of piety is a bloodsucking traitor who works for the occupying authorities, and the bad example is a respected theologian who goes to church twice a week. Perhaps the only genuine example story in Jesus' repertoire is the parable of the Rich Fool in Luke 12:16–21, about whom Jesus seems to be saying, "There is no mystery here:

35

this is precisely the sort of person you should *not* become, and exactly the foolish behavior you should avoid at all costs."

In *The Gospel of Thomas*, a gnostic gospel of unknown provenance and date (most, though not all, estimates range from 140–200 CE), the fifteen parables attributed to Jesus are closest to example stories in form and function, that is, parables from which allegorical explanations and even metaphorical "puzzles" are missing or have been removed. This gospel consists entirely of logia (sayings) with no narrative of Jesus' ministry, death, and resurrection (Nicholas Perrin, *Thomas: The Other Gospel*, 73–139). The following are representative examples of the numbered logia:

> And he [Jesus] said, "Humankind is like a wise fisherman who cast his net into the sea and drew it up from the sea full of little fish. Among them the wise fisherman discovered a fine large fish. He threw all the little fish back into the sea and with no difficulty chose the large fish. Whoever has ears to hear should hear."
>
> (*Thomas* 8)

> Jesus said, "The kingdom is like a person who had a hidden treasure in his field but did not know it. And [when] he died, he left it to his [son]. The son [did] not know [about it]. He took over the field and sold it. The buyer went plowing, [discovered] the treasure, and began to lend money at interest to whomever he wished."
>
> (*Thomas* 109)

Since so many questions remain concerning this gospel's relation to the canonical Gospels, it is difficult to know how to use *The Gospel of Thomas* in relation to the parables of Jesus. For our purposes, it is enough to say that this is what a parable looks like when its revelatory, metaphorical element is flattened and the saying is orphaned from its home in the biblical narrative. It enters the realm of *advice*, which, when it comes to popular opinion of the parables, is a genre with which we are familiar.

3. *Allegory* is an ancient strategy of communication. It functions by pointing away from the story or parable toward "other" (Greek *allos*) values that lie outside the story. Allegory was sometimes used apologetically in an effort to find a higher meaning in a text, as in the Greek philosophers who allegorized the sexual and brutal scenes in Homer. Others, such as the philosopher Philo, the first-century Hellenistic Jew, understood allegory's capacity

for reconciling antithetical worldviews and used it to harmonize the Old Testament with Greek philosophy. The medieval church employed allegory as a method of imparting to the faithful the biblical text's fullest doctrinal and ecclesial significance, its *sensus plenior*. In the parlance of allegory, *didactic* is not a bad word!

The allegorist reasons in the following manner: Since the Scriptures are of divine authorship, why would God's Word restrict itself to historical truths—thin and malleable *facts*—without making available the fullness of the divine life as it is revealed in the church's doctrines and practices? Far from an interpretative add-on or arbitrary technique, allegory provides indispensable testimony to the richness of God's written Word.

The best-known "modern" example of allegory is John Bunyan's *Pilgrim's Progress* (1678), in which every character and situation stands for extratextual Christian values. The reader experiences a certain comforting delight in the one-for-one correspondences between Hopeful, Mr. Sagacity, Pliable, Mr. Implacable, Doubting Castle, the Slough of Despond—and their doctrinal and moral counterparts.

We shall return to allegory in the next chapter in our discussion of Mark 4:13–20 and 12:1–2, but before we leave it, let me give a more recent example of a genre that has maintained its hold on the contemporary imagination. Some years ago I attended a German performance of Bertholt Brecht's *The Resistible Rise of Arturo Ui* (1941), a play that chronicles the ascendency of a Chicago gangster modeled after the infamous Al Capone. The first act was pure melodrama, as buffoonish mobsters with their tommy guns and zoot suits took over the city and its neighboring communities through intimidation and terrorism, which included the firebombing of a warehouse. The audience loved it. In the second act the same actors appeared, but now they were goose-stepping and saluting one another. The Al Capone figure was wearing a small moustache, and it was not difficult to pick out Goering and Goebbels and others in the Nazi hierarchy. The burning Chicago warehouse was no longer a warehouse but the German Reichstag. The audience sat in silence throughout the second act, and no one laughed.

From this experience we might draw two conclusions. Allegory is more than a teaching tool; it is capable of operating on a more intense emotional level than the intellectual or didactic. Everyone in the theater was familiar with the legendary Chicago mobsters, and everyone

37

knew about Hitler's rise to power. The portrayal of Hitler and his associates as gangsters was not educational, but transformational. In this instance, allegory functioned with the potency of metaphor. Second, the power of any figure of speech, including an allegory, depends on the audience. How much does the audience already know? What were its expectations when it came to the theater or opened the book? Is it still capable of being surprised, shocked, or moved by this material? Ultimately, it is the audience that grants to the allegory its aesthetic viability, and it is the audience that decides if it will be educated, amused, bored, shocked, confirmed, or transformed by what it sees on the stage, hears from the pulpit, or reads in the book.

We began this section by alluding to some of the shortcomings of theological and literary classification. Let me deepen that warning by commenting on a more serious problem related to parable research. From all indications, Jesus used parables to confront and convict his generation. The kingdom he proclaimed was not an idea but a force intended to move his hearers from an old way of life to a radically new one. Everything about his parables points to their illocutionary thrust: they are stories of intent. Moreover, the simplicity of their design and the universality of their message reveal an inherently forward purpose, that of illumining new generations and penetrating new contexts. A great deal of biblical scholarship, however, has limited itself to historical questions and literary classification, thereby slighting something fundamental to the nature of the parables. Whenever we fail to ask what a parable *means*—present tense—can we claim to have interpreted the parable?

Joachim Jeremias's groundbreaking work on the historical context of the parables tells us virtually everything we can possibly know about what Jesus' parables meant to the early community and the Synoptic evangelists, but absolutely nothing about what they mean to us. The German edition of his book *The Parables of Jesus* appeared in 1947, a scant two years after the end of World War II. It was entangled in its own context of unprecedented moral, political, and ecclesial crisis (Oldenhage, *Parables for Our Time: Rereading New Testament Scholarship after the Holocaust*, 39–59, passim). Great crimes had been committed against the Jewish people; Germany and the German church lay in ruins; suffering, death, and judgment were everywhere. Perhaps the exegete is not the self-appointed preacher to his readers, but when sifting through texts that, *by their very nature*, claim relevance to the crisis moment in which life hangs in the balance, doesn't the reader deserve a new word about the present context? What might the parables of the Two Sons, the Laborers in the Vineyard, or the Wicked Tenants—colored as they are by the troubled relationship of Judaism and early followers of Jesus—say to post-Holocaust Christians who, despite the abject failure of the church, continue to claim pride of place in the kingdom of God? After Auschwitz, how was it possible for Jeremias to write on "The Imminence of Catastrophe" without so much as alluding to the catastrophe that had befallen European Jews and his homeland, Germany? How was it possible for him to speak of the Jews in the New Testament as a "blinded people" and "a nation rushing upon its own destruction" without reflecting on the terrible irony of such judgments? (Jeremias, *Parables of Jesus*, 160, 169; Oldenhage, *Parables for Our Time*, 51–53).

T. S. Eliot writes in "Little Gidding": "For last year's words belong to last year's language / And next year's words await another voice." The genuinely new voice that emerged from Germany after World War II was not the chorus of famous historical critics who introduced generations of seminarians to the "science" of biblical interpretation. Rather, it was the voice of preachers like Martin Niemöller, Hermann Maas, and Helmut Thielicke, and the Dutch evangelist Corrie ten Boom, who proclaimed the kingdom of God. In the decade after the war, the preacher and theologian Helmut Thielicke attracted enormous crowds to St. Michael's Church in Hamburg with his sermons on the parables of Jesus. It was Thielicke who, in the shattered context of postwar Germany, when so many others remained silent, powerfully transmitted the parables' message of crisis, judgment, and hope. About his own sermons the preacher wrote, "The language of preaching, which must dispense with all qualifying and safeguarding clauses and is essentially decisive, has cost the author far more effort and trouble than 'carpentered' academic forms of speech" (*Waiting Father*, 13, my trans.). In the crisis moment, Paul's question rang clear: "And how are they to hear [the word of God] without a preacher?" (Rom. 10:14 RSV).

Social Setting

A final classification pays close attention to the social setting of the parables of Jesus. Categories such as village versus urban life, family dynamics versus the political sphere; master's rights versus slave vulnerability—all these have been employed by a growing number of scholars. Their interests represent attempts to correct the abstract and spiritual approaches of theological interpretation. Luise Schottroff announces that in her book "the text of the New Testament is located not only in terms of its intellectual history but also and above all in its *social history*, and is questioned with regard to the praxis of life that is bound up with it" (*Parables of Jesus*, 1). In the mid-1970s Kenneth Bailey was laying the groundwork for this concern with his "Oriental exegesis" and his assertion that the parables of Jesus cannot be understood apart from peasant life in Galilean villages, vestiges of which survive to this day (*Poet and Peasant*). Thirty years earlier Joachim Jeremias had already taught us a great deal about the social milieu of first-century Palestine, but scholars such as Schottroff, Bernard Brandon Scott, and William Herzog have taken contextualization to a new level by making it the *basis* of parable interpretation. They have interrogated the "fathers" of parable scholarship, for whom the point of most parables consists in a theological solution to problems faced by Jesus' community or the early church, and have offered another sort of reading.

The social-critical interpreters have shifted the bottom line of Jesus' parables—the "answer," one might say—from a theological exposition of the kingdom to an *intervention* in the social lives and structures of the community (see chap. 5 below). They do not understand themselves as mere interpreters of the parables, but as interpreters of the contemporary world *by means of* the parables. Now understood as "codifications" of social conditions, Jesus' stories have been given a new platform from which to explore a range of power relations in the world. Critical comments on politics, economics, and sexuality are no longer construed as "applications" drawn from background or incidental conditions suggested by the parables; rather, it was (and is) the mission of the parables both to address and change the conditions themselves.

How does the approach of the sociocritical interpreters differ from Thielicke's gospel-centered preaching? It is a fair question since both address situations of social devastation. The answer lies in their respective starting points. Social contextualists start with the problem and seek redress from many sources, including secular analysis and a prophetic reading of the Bible. Thielicke begins with revelation and finds sufficient resources in its theological message

40

to address persons in spiritual, psychological, and economic distress. In the contextual approach, sociopolitical and economic considerations are taken into the fabric of the scriptural word itself. The spiritual or theological orientation of its central message, be it the kingdom of God or redemption through the cross, is abolished in favor of a rereading of the New Testament that engages structures of injustice, whether in ancient Palestine or the contemporary world. The social critic reads the New Testament by means of social, political, and economic theory. Although both critical approaches address situations of social upheaval or inequality, in Thielicke's theological reading the message of God's kingdom offers an implicit judgment of abusive power. Like Karl Barth, who challenged the Nazis by proclaiming "Jesus is Lord," Thielicke relies on the inherent power of the message to illumine a new way for the people of God. Herzog and Schottroff, though not known as political activists, read the story of Jesus "politically" as a resource and ally in the transformation of unjust societies.

CHAPTER 2

Four Theories for Reading
the Parables

From the beginning, the parables of Jesus gave rise to multiple interpretations. His stories were so varied in literary form, so rooted in
religious communities, so embedded in specific social conditions, and
(most of all) so mysterious in their intent—it was inevitable that they
would lead readers in many directions. In this chapter we will limit
ourselves to four distinct theories of reading the parables of Jesus.

Theory I: Parables Obscure the Truth

They intend to explain nothing. The fourth chapter of the Gospel
of Mark opens with a parable of planting and growth. The character who tells the story is an itinerating healer named Jesus, whom
the evangelist has already identified in Mark 1:1 with the headline,
"Christ [the anointed one], the Son of God." The authority of this
teller of stories has already been attested from every conceivable
direction: from the Scriptures, by a voice at his baptism, by the
leading prophet of his day, by a leper, and even by a demon who
delivers the most powerful witness of all: "I know who you are, the
Holy One of God" (Mark 1:24), a confession that his comrades from
the underworld will repeat in Mark 3:11 and 5:7.   43
     The crowd also plays a significant role in its appraisal of Jesus.
The many people he has cured, as well as hordes of the curious, are

so great that they threaten to "crush him." For that reason he first escapes to the mountains to gather his disciples and from there travels to his home in Capernaum, where the surge of people is so insistent, the narrator says, he "could not even eat" (Mark 3:20). The scribes accuse him of being a devil, to which Jesus replies "in parables," but not initially in the short-story form we have come to identify as "parable," but with *mĕšālîm* characteristic of the Hebrew prophets: "How can Satan cast out Satan? . . . But no one can enter a strong man's house and plunder his property without first tying up the strong man" (Mark 3:23b, 27). Finally he has no choice but to board a boat and from there teach the multitude gathered on the shore.

From a narrative point of view, what he says from the boat comes as something of an anticlimax. He begins to tell parables, this time not in pithy, sentifentious riddles but in the form of narratives, a genre of teaching with which his eager listeners would have been less familiar. Surrounded by the symbols and paraphernalia of fishing, he tells an unexceptional story drawn from the world of agriculture (Mark 4:1–9). It will prove to be the programmatic parable of his ministry.

A sower went out to sow, but, due to the birds, the scorching sun, and thorns, the seed yields nothing on the first three tries. However some of the seed falls on "good soil" (notice, it's not the seed whose quality varies, but the soil), and it brings forth—and here is the surprising part of the story—a graduated yield of thirty-fold, sixtyfold, and a hundredfold (cf. Gen. 26:12), more than several times the expected yield. That's it.

As it stands, this little story makes narrative sense only in light of the auspicious beginning of Jesus' ministry. But the narrator of the Gospel (not to be confused with the author, "Mark") as well as the main character portrayed in it (Jesus) know more than can possibly be revealed at this point in the narrative. The parable appears to anticipate both a bountiful return from the ministry of Jesus *and* the possibility of disappointing results. With its threefold pattern of failure, the parable hints at difficulties and disappointments ahead. While some commentators have focused on the contrast between the smallness of the seed and the abundance of the harvest, the insignificance of the seed is not emphasized here as it is in the parable of the Mustard Seed later in the chapter. In fact, there is an abundance of seed; the seed is not the problem. The sower

44

broadcasts it in the most inhospitable places and in every conceivable zone of human life. What exactly the seed "stands for" is not divulged in the parable; nor do any values representing repentance, belief, Satan, or temptation make an obvious appearance. The parable does not focus on the goodness or other personal qualities of the sower; he is identified only as a "sower," without the endearing grace of a waiting father or a loving shepherd. As the parable proceeds, the sower gradually (and grammatically) recedes from view: "Other seed fell. . . ." Having introduced Jesus to the reader and demonstrated his authority in the first three chapters, the narrative now turns its attention to the audience.

The core of the original parable emphasizes the importance of reception, specifically, the response to Jesus' performance of the kingdom. Jesus portrays the sower and the act of sowing in impersonal and mechanical terms, but he pointedly foreshadows the receivers' response, first in the three failures of the seed to germinate, then in the gradations of the soil's productivity.

At last we begin to see the importance of "the crowd" that has followed him from place to place, hounded him into the boat, and now listens to his message from the shore. The crowd is not a prop or an artificial means of inflating Jesus' fame. In this story, it will be the crowd's job to respond as representatives of Israel, and it will be from the crowd that Jesus will quickly cull the true responders who are capable of producing a yield of abundant discipleship and suffering. Already in this optimistic parable of growth, then, we see the unmistakable shadows of attrition. With the teacher sequestered in the boat, "the crowd" is necessarily detached from him on the shore. The crowd is physically and, to the reader's eye, visually separated from him; unlike his closest followers, the crowd will never enjoy the intimacy of being "with him." The multitude that was once so great that it threatened "to crush" him will later in the narrative do just that: "So the crowd came and began to ask Pilate to do for them according to his custom" (Mark 15:8).

The next scene, then, does not come as a great surprise. When he is "alone" and away from the crowd, the small group of true responders asks him about the parables. Verses 3–9 have prepared us for his summary of their content: "the secret [*mystērion*] of the kingdom of God." Anticipating his own rejection, Jesus unveils another, deeper mystery of the kingdom when he divulges the true purpose of his parables, which is not to illustrate the truth but to

45

obscure it. He freely quotes Isaiah 6, the call of Isaiah, whose rejection was also anticipated: in order that (Greek *hina*)

> "they may indeed look but not perceive
> And may indeed listen, but not understand;
> so that they may not [*mēpote* = lest] turn again
> and be forgiven."
>
> (Mark 4:12)

The people's rejection of God's servant is unforgivable—at least, for now. So unfathomably deep is the rejection that, just as unfathomably, God wills their blindness, deafness, and hardness of heart, which are the physical symbols of unbelief. This is a hard saying. Mark reproduces Isaiah's use of the intensive "as they look, seeing, they will not perceive" and "as they listen, hearing, they will not understand," the force of which in several translations is weakly conveyed by the word "indeed." Given what follows in the Gospel, one can only conclude that Jesus or the early community conceived the words of Isaiah as the divine premise of every rebellion and rejection that would follow: the very act of rejecting God's servant constitutes the punishment itself and confirms God's judgment. "For to those who have, more will be given; and from those who have nothing [e.g., faith], even what they have will be taken away" (Mark 4:25).

One might ask, What can be taken away from a person who has nothing? Is this a case of predestination? Or is there a tiny worm of unbelief from the beginning that only God can see and punish in advance? The questions and rationalizations pile up into an unedifying heap. Human reason reacts to these verses either with revulsion, as in the case of Albert Schweitzer, who found such sentiments "repellent," or with disbelief that a loving and merciful Savior could have uttered them. There must be some mistake! The literary critic Frank Kermode has addressed the issue in *The Genesis of Secrecy*, but his response merely shifts the mystery from the nature of God to the nature of narrative. When it comes to the interpretation of texts, Kermode argues, we are all outsiders: "Mark is a strong witness to the enigmatic and exclusive character of narrative, to its property of banishing interpreters from its secret places" 46 (*Genesis of Secrecy*, 33–34). He goes on to say, rightly, that even the "insiders" in this story, the disciples, prove to be hopeless outsiders when it comes to understanding the words of Jesus.

But this saying in Mark 4:11–12 is not so much a hermeneutical problem as it is a divine mystery. This is God's way, and no one can understand it: not Isaiah, not the evangelist Mark, and not even Paul, who in Romans 11 similarly attributes Israel's rejection of Jesus to a hardening and a "sluggish spirit" sent by God. The double ray of hope and warning coming from Paul might guide our reading of this difficult passage as well: In Romans, Paul is confident that the positions of those who have accepted and/or rejected the gospel are not fixed for all eternity; just as God was able to graft the Gentiles into the tree of salvation, God is able to break them off again. And just as God was able to cut off those to whom had been given the covenants, the law, the glory, and the promises (Rom. 9:4), God is able regraft them into the tree of life (Rom. 11:11–15, 29). In other words, as dire as Isaiah and Mark's theory of the word might appear, the diagnosis may not be permanent. Indeed, as Joel Marcus points out, "In Isaiah, Mark's source, a whole series of later texts (29:18, 24; 32:3; 35:5) implies that the new age will bring a reversal of the sentence of insensibility found in Isaiah 6 . . ." (*Mark 1–8,* 307).

Does the theory of parable found in the Gospel of Mark originate with Jesus or the early church? Jesus does not explain his comment in Mark 4:11–12 or elaborate his motive in making it; therefore it is tempting to view Theory I, "Parables Obscure the Truth," as a Marcan construction used by the evangelist to complement Jesus' commands of secrecy and to explain his rejection by "those outside." But given that a divinely induced mode of rejection had already found expression in the Scriptures, it is not inconceivable that early in his ministry Jesus himself viewed his parables as instruments of his Father's wrath. In either case, in Mark's Gospel the parables are meant to obscure. And if this is true, the little metaphors that Jesus expanded into narratives have themselves become metaphors of their inevitable rejection—of the trivial, superficial, manipulative, and ignorant uses to which the parables have been subjected over the centuries. Given that the creature has (at least in its own eyes) displaced the Creator, how else can one grasp the enormity of the sin unless one sees God's hand in God's own rejection? How else to read the impending catastrophe than "It was meant to be"?

That Matthew changes the purposive *hina* for a conjunction denoting cause, *hoti* ("because"), doesn't do much to relieve the pain because we still have the quotation from Isaiah to deal with,

47

the thrust of which has to do with God's imposition of unbelief on the ears and hearts of those to whom his prophet will speak. It is true that Matthew (13:15) drops the word "lest" out of the quotation from Isaiah, and that in his Gospel the words of the prophet are not attributed to Jesus but to the evangelist's own summary of the passage in Isaiah. And even if the Aramaic word for "lest" can be translated "unless," as Jeremias assures us, thereby shifting responsibility for unbelief from God to the hearers, the unmistakable spirit of the Isaiah passage remains (*Parables of Jesus*, 17). For if one does not believe that God is in some measure hardening hearts and obscuring the truth, there is no reason to quote the passage at all.

Jesus' theory of parable as articulated by the evangelist Mark is not so much perverse as it is tragic. It is published at a historical moment when the evangelist has already seen the future. He knows what Jesus might well have anticipated, that the message of the kingdom will be deployed in a fog of rejection, disappointment, and unfulfilled eschatological hopes. The evangelist's theory of parable cannot be refuted on the basis of the parables in Mark 4, where even the programmatic parable of the Sower elicits misunderstanding (but by the disciples in 4:13) and raises forebodings of bad things to come. The pervasive ignorance and the disciples' need for private tutoring will continue throughout Mark's Gospel (cf. Mark 7:17–23; 13:28). Mark's theory breaks down definitively, however, in the Gospels of Matthew and Luke, where Jesus tells his parables openly for the purpose of instructing or reproving all who hear them. Far from being dark or obscure, in these Gospels the parables are lighted lamps along the path of the kingdom.

Theory II: Parables Teach Many Truths

An obscure agricultural parable is followed by an even more obscure rationale for speaking in parables, and then, almost magically, the mystery is cleared up in a few sentences. The miracle worker turns teacher, offers a brief seminar in hermeneutics, and decodes his own parable.

If there is a constant connecting the original parable, the rationale from Isaiah 6, and the explanation of the parable in Mark

4:13–20, it is to be found in the response of the hearers. Otherwise the entire chapter cuts from scene to scene like impressionistic fiction or a badly edited film: Jesus is in the boat, then out of it with his disciples; then in verse 35 he is back in the boat again, and with each move his style of speaking and the composition of the audience change. In verses 13–20, many of his expressions, such as, "the word" for preaching, the receiving of it "with joy," "persecution," "cares of the world," and "the lure of wealth" seem more at home in the apostolic church than on the lips of Jesus. The explanation of his parable abruptly turns our attention from the mystery of the kingdom to the psychology of unbelief.

And yet, the explanation is true! One can be so distracted by the apparent linguistic inconsistencies of verses 13–20 as to overlook the empirical realism of the allegory. If the rationale drawn from Isaiah stretches our credulity to the breaking point, the explanation of the parable rings true to every generation. The allegorical method of explaining the original parable, in which many of the details of the story stand for truths already known to the reader, confirms the church's experience of every age. Preaching the word *is* like sowing seeds in harsh and uncertain conditions (cf. Isa. 55:10–11). The preacher puts it out there, unsure of who is listening and who is not, unable to calibrate the sermon to its "target audience," and *never* able to predict its outcome. Sadly, the word does *not* take root in many cases and is choked by the cares of the world and the lure of wealth. How many missionaries and church workers have looked back on decades of work only to hear the mordant echo of verse 19: "and it yields *nothing*"?

Twenty-first-century congregations, whose members know very little about the uncertainties of farming, still pray for a bountiful harvest as they sing their eucharistic liturgies,

> Let the vineyards be fruitful, Lord,
> And fill to the brim our cup of blessing.
> Gather a harvest from the seeds that were sown,
> That we may be fed with the bread of life.

In this particular offertory, the seeds that have been sown stand for the reading and preaching of the word of God. It continues by relating the metaphor of sowing and ingathering to the hopes, dreams, and prayers of God's people, who are now preparing to be fed from that which has been harvested:

49

Gather the hopes and dreams of all;
unite them with the prayers we offer.
Grace our table with your presence,
And give us a foretaste of the feast to come.
(*Evangelical Lutheran Worship* [2006])

The biblical text teaches everything, because every passage is a pod filled with the seeds of truth. Two theological convictions undergird the church's use of allegory: First, the true author of Scripture is God, whose eternal purposes transcend the historical moments in which the word was uttered and the text produced. So much so that in Thomas Aquinas the "literal" meaning of a passage is not limited to the historical intent of its author, but to every truth God intends for humanity and the church. That capacious understanding of "literal" has been severely curtailed by modern "literalism."

As a genre, allegory tends to create new audiences. Diachronically—that is, through time—God's word gathers what the literary critic John Ciardi called a "vertical audience" of unimagined number and complexity. Allegory envisions a truth so large that it encompasses the divine author, human writers and editors, the original recipients, and the church of every age. "Scripture" is no longer a collection of texts, but the enveloping context in which believers live and worship.

A second theological conviction motivates the Christian embrace of allegory: the resurrection of Jesus. Already in the Gospel accounts, the truth and power of his resurrection produces the inevitable hermeneutical aftershocks. The following is always a valid question: Would this parable have any claim on us if Jesus Christ were not raised from the dead? The answer is no, but the effective mechanism by which the risen Christ informs our reading of his earthly parables is not entirely clear.

The resurrection of Jesus energizes faithful reading in many practical ways. For example, the resurrection entails a deeper and more courageous commitment on the part of the interpreter to the transformation of the very contexts in which the parable is read. Participants in cell groups and base communities, prison and hospital chaplains, parents instructing children, and many others have interpreted the parables by making them vehicles of good news in situations of oppression or sadness. Their readings, too, spring

50

from the resurrection of Jesus. The witness of the women on Easter morning, "We have seen the Lord," need not be limited to the record of a small group's experience of something called "resurrection." The contemporary reader may join in their confession and participate in their joy, with the result that "We have seen the Lord" crashes through the subject-object barrier that separates the contemporary reader from the written text. Historical-critical interpretation understands after the flesh; but because the Spirit of the risen One fills the world, the church now reads from the perspective of the Holy Spirit's many gifts to the people of God. The allegorical method of interpretation is but one way believers in Jesus celebrate the triumph of God in the resurrection of the Son.

A great deal of parable interpretation, however, presumes that, as a genre or a strategy of communication, allegory is inferior to simple storytelling or what is often designated as "true parable." Not only does the presence of allegory suggest the church's hand in altering the stories Jesus told, but it is also claimed that allegory's didacticism makes for a less satisfying literary experience. Allegory, it is argued, requires very little creativity on the part of the author and leaves even less to the imagination of the reader. It is easy to fall into a snobbish mind-set based on current literary tastes. The contributions of allegory invite the contemporary reader to join the great company of interpreters. We enjoy a latter-day fellowship with Irenaeus, Origen, Jerome, Augustine, the Venerable Bede, Gregory the Great, Bernard of Clairvaux, and all the rest, and benefit from their faithful and creative methods of interpretation. Likewise, the history of literature is too long and rich for us to dismiss Plato's *Republic*, *Pilgrim's Progress*, *Gulliver's Travels*, *The Scarlet Letter*, *Moby Dick*, *The Chronicles of Narnia*, *The Wizard of Oz*, *The Crucible*, *Fahrenheit 451*, *Lord of the Flies*, *The Name of the Rose*, *Star Wars*, and *Harry Potter* for the allegorical elements found in them.

No matter the critical prejudice against allegory, we cannot overlook the many allegorical features of the parables of Jesus. It's hard to find what Dan O. Via refers to as "autotelic" art in the New Testament, that is, stories whose meaning or purpose is not driven by Jesus' or his community's desire to instruct, correct, warn, or otherwise signal a truth that extends beyond the fictive world of the story (*The Parables*, 78–88). Three parables—the Sower, the Weeds among the Wheat, and the Net (the last two only in Matthew)—have allegorical explanations appended to them.

51

Only one parable, the Wicked Tenants (Mark 12:1–12//Matt. 21:33–46//Luke 20:9–19) qualifies as a self-contained allegory. In it the "beloved son" (in Mark and Luke only) and the other characters clearly represent dramatis personae in the history of salvation culminating in the crucifixion of the Son. The parable is strategically placed in all three Gospels as the gateway to the passion of the Son. It is a rare example of a rabbinic-style parable that explicates a Scripture, in this case, Isaiah's Song of the Vineyard: "Let me sing for my beloved my love-song concerning his vineyard . . ." (Isa. 5:1–7). Jesus' parable expands the reference in Isaiah by suggesting that the wicked tenants are planning to displace the owner and claim the vineyard as their own possession, which effectively adds idolatry to their list of sins.

The tenants represent the leaders of Judaism in Jesus' day. They mistreat three slaves in succession, who call to mind the prophets, about whom Jesus once predicted, "I send you prophets, sages, and scribes, some of whom you will kill and crucify" (Matt. 23:34a). The vineyard is littered with the bodies of the prophets. But the treatment of the final messenger, the beloved son, is given the fullest detailing, including the use of dialogue ("This is the heir; come, let us kill him") and the owner's internal monologue ("They will respect ['reverence' KJV] my son"), all of which invests the story with a pathos not usually encountered in allegory. The owner determines the action, but the climax of the story belongs to the son. Given the long-suffering hope of the vineyard owner, about whom only late in the story do we learn that he even *has* a son, the parable might be titled "The Naive Father." Finally, the last movement in the parable highlights the perfidy of the "wicked tenants," whose motives and violent methods are thoroughly exposed. In the remainder of chapter 12, Mark cleverly reintroduces his readers to the "tenants": in rapid succession he brings them back on stage one last time in the costume of Pharisees, Herodians, Sadducees, and scribes, each of whom makes a cameo appearance in conflict with Jesus.

The parable appears in Matthew and Luke with relatively minor alterations, with the exception of Matthew's coda in which Jesus predicts the ultimate consequences of the tenants' revolt: "Therefore I tell you, the kingdom of God will be taken away from you and given to a people that produces the fruits of the kingdom" (Matt. 21:43). This is characteristic of Matthew's more comprehensive theology of replacement and succession with regard to those who either accept or reject the ministry of Jesus. The critical tone of the parable vis-à-vis Israel's past failures is somewhat moderated by the "you" in verse 43, which suggests that the audience for his parables in the temple is "the chief priests and elders of the people" (21:23) whose hostility toward Jesus is contrasted with the crowds, who regarded him as a prophet (21:45–46).

Many interpreters have insisted that the earthly Jesus could not have performed the allegory of the Wicked Tenants in his own voice. With its many apostolic markers, the parable has a decidedly retrospective cast and reflects the faith of the primitive Christian community. There is a point to these observations, but we should not rush to judgment. We might also ask the following questions and admit that the answer to each of them is yes: Could the historical Jesus have possibly understood the conflicts engendered by his ministry in terms of Isaiah's Song of the Vineyard (Isa. 5), verses known to every student of the Scriptures? Could the one who addressed God as Abba have possibly referred to himself as a son or even a "beloved son"? (Mark 12:6). Could the messianic figure who has been prophesying his own death since early in his ministry have possibly guessed that he would be seized and killed? Even if the more obvious allegorical markers are the work of a later community, which seems likely, the above questions demonstrate more continuity than discontinuity between the historical Jesus and the primitive church's assessment of him. (For a nonallegorical reading of the Wicked Tenants, see the discussion in chap. 5, "Reading the Parables with the Poor").

We must also take note of the elements of allegory in many other parables. The various parables of preparedness found in Matthew 24 and 25—the Thief in the Night, the Faithful and Wicked Slaves, the Bridesmaids, the Talents—are not allegorical in every detail—for example, the "talent" might mean many things—but they are best read as allegories of Christ's return. They have two basic messages: the master will return at an unexpected hour; therefore, be ready! It is easy to imagine these parables on the lips of Jesus, perhaps not as warnings of his return on the last day, but as alarums calling attention to the crisis of the kingdom of God. Seen in this way, the parables of preparedness mirror Jesus' surprising entry onto the historical stage in Mark 1 and the astonishment evoked by his mighty works. Just as the parables of preparedness

53

posit two types of response to the return of the master, so Jesus' sudden appearance in Galilee also evokes a dual reaction: some oppose and torment him; others receive him with hospitality, faith, and discipleship.

We may consider a final example of allegory in the parable of the Great Feast found in Luke 14:16–24 and Matthew 22:1–14. Perhaps no other parable offers a clearer example of allegorical technique than Matthew's treatment of the material he held in common with Luke. The key to the difference between these two versions of the same story lies in the writers' theological purpose. (At the outset, let us be clear that contrary to later Christian moralistic preaching, neither version of the parable is about making excuses for one's lack of involvement in church activities!)

In his account, Luke portrays Jesus as one whose ministry invites outcasts to the kingdom. It fits nicely with the extended image of the wedding banquet in the previous verses, about which Jesus says it is better to start in the cheap seats and be invited to the place of honor with the words, "Friend, move up higher" (Luke 14:10). Where Luke's parable captures the core dynamic of the kingdom, Matthew's aspires to a grander and more global summation. His version of the parable encompasses nothing less than the clearly demarcated history of divine salvation. Luke's story leads to the "gospel within the Gospel" of Luke 15; Matthew's leads to rejection by the religious leaders and the tragedy of the passion.

The protagonist is a "man" in Luke but a "king" in Matthew; Luke's "great banquet" is Matthew's "marriage feast," a Christian image for the messianic banquet promised in Isaiah 25:6. Luke's singular servant is made plural in Matthew ("other servants," 22:4 RSV), signifying the various dispensations and repudiations of the prophets. In Matthew's version the rejection goes well beyond excuses: they "seized his servants, treated them shamefully, and killed them" (Matt. 22:6 RSV). The king responds in kind by sending troops and burning the city, an *ex eventu* reference to the Roman destruction of Jerusalem. Finally, Luke's version concludes with a houseful of new invitees along with the warning that those originally summoned will not taste the banquet. In Matthew the hall is also filled but with guests "both bad and good," no doubt a reflection of his Gospel's preoccupation with the purity of the community.

54

Matthew's version of the parable of the Great Feast reflects the circumstances of two distinct conflicts swirling around his community: With a few simple strokes, Matthew ratchets up the conflict with the religious authorities, justifying both the destruction of Jerusalem and the initiative toward the Gentiles, *and* in the same parable lays the groundwork for an intramural theological conflict over the composition of the Christian community (cf. the Weeds among the Wheat). The parable form allows him to pursue his theological agenda with great economy. He does not need to write treatises and sermons on the matters that trouble him, but by means of a few deft (some would say "heavy-handed") strokes of the quill, the allegory of the Great Feast does the job for him.

Paradoxically, however, only Matthew brings a genuine sense of drama to what in both Gospels is a highly stylized story. The drama occurs at the end, after Luke's parable is finished, when the king appears and enters the packed hall and notices a man who is improperly dressed. Since this episode is not merely a tag end to the allegory, but represents a separate, nonallegorical scene, we will consider it later, in a section on the literary reading of parables.

Finally, what about the allegorical interpretation of parables from which the obvious markers are missing? It is one thing to acknowledge and learn from allegory; it is quite another to *allegorize* nonallegorical parables in order to produce meanings that are not there. For most of its history the church has disregarded the distinction between *allegory* and *allegorize*. Jülicher was right: allegory can get out of hand; when it does, it interferes with the commonsense reading of the text and, instead of enhancing its richness, distorts its meaning. Jesus' questions—"What is written? How do you read?"—not only incriminate the historical critics of Scripture, but also the practitioners of theological exegesis who allow their ecclesial commitments to override the plain sense of the text. Both the higher critics and the theological interpreters make a valid point: not one of Jesus' parables conveys a meaning wholly internal to itself without reference to a historical or theological reality. Any narrative asks, Why? To what end? Even art that has no redeeming social purpose is intent on expressing *something*. But such observations do not constitute a license to read a moral or religious value *into* the text.

Luke 11:5–8 is the parable of the Friend at Midnight. It tells about an ordinary person ("one of you") who goes to a "friend" at midnight and asks for three loaves of bread. The friend inside the house irritably replies, "'Do not bother me; the door has already been locked, and my children are with me in bed.'" Jesus concludes, "I tell you, even though he will not get up and give him anything because he is a friend, at least because of his persistence he will get up and give him whatever he needs." Despite its unambiguous teaching on persistence in prayer, the parable of the Friend at Midnight has been allegorized to yield a plethora of Christian truths. In one of his sermons on this passage (Sermon 105 in *Patrologiae cursus completus, series Latina*, in Wailes, *Medieval Allegories of Jesus' Parables*, 215–17), Augustine describes the person knocking on the door as someone who is exhausted by worldliness. The roadway from which he comes is the evil life of the world. The midnight hour signifies the crisis of the soul, a time when the prophets, Peter, and Paul are no longer available to help. We (in the audience) cannot feed him because our faith is too simple. But when he turns to his friend, whom Augustine identifies in this sermon as the Scriptures, he receives what he needs: sustenance in his knowledge of the Trinity. In a later work, *Questions on the Gospels*, Augustine refines his interpretation of the man in need, who he says symbolizes an aspect of our human nature, our appetitive desire (col. 1341, Wailes 217). Knowledge of the Trinity is expressed by obtaining three things of the same substance, the three loaves, which, though white, brown, and barley, are all bread and signify one triune substance (cf. Augustine, *Essential Sermons*, 166).

Augustine's reading, minus its Trinitarian focus, was amplified by Martin Luther King Jr. in his flagship sermon "A Knock at Midnight." In that sermon he uses "midnight" in three senses, the social, moral, and individual order; the knock at the door is the world's cry for help; the house stands for the church; and the three loaves of bread represent faith, hope, and love. The householder's reluctance to answer represents the church's preoccupation with its own affairs above its concern for those in need (*A Knock at Midnight*, 65–83). King's sermon is every bit as allegorical as anything the ancient or medieval church ever produced. It is a reminder that allegory need not merely maintain the status quo but can serve as an instrument of moral and social awakening.

Augustine's reading was appropriated by many of the church's teachers and preachers. Most modern interpretations appear arid in comparison. The problem with allegorical interpretation is the problem of the theological scope of interpretation (which I will

56

consider later) and its authority. Who decides what it *means?* Is it the *church* whose doctrine and doctors provide a series of lenses through which believers read the text? Or is it the modern institution of "higher criticism," which is often as interested in the *world* that produced the text as it is in the text itself? The *text* is the only suitable platform for a hermeneutical debate. Neither the church's many-sided tradition nor critical theory has the authority to override the clear sense of the words on the page, which is indicated by many factors, including the passage's function within the theological purpose of the Gospel. Ironically, at both ends of the interpretive spectrum—the ecclesial and the social/contextual—a word of Scripture is subjected to extratextual agendas.

But Luke has a context too. He places the parable in the narrative environment of Jesus' teaching on prayer. "Give us each day our daily bread" (Luke 11:3) has echoes in the traveler's request for three loaves of bread. Following the parable, Jesus' explanation is perfectly consistent with the content of the parable itself until, perhaps, his mention of the Holy Spirit in verse 13, which introduces a new dimension to what has been a discussion of prayer as a persistent asking. Thus the parable, which has no parallels or comparable contexts, simply stands as a teaching on one facet of prayer, and one that is organically related to Luke's Gospel: God knows what you need; to those who ask, he will give the ultimate gift, the gift of the Holy Spirit.

In two of his sermons, Augustine looks beyond the clear sense of the parable in order to make other points, most of which cannot be documented from the text except by reference to church doctrine and philosophy. Christians do believe in the tripartite personhood and substantial unity of the Holy Trinity, and with the help of Plato and others, we do understand humanity's appetitive nature. But the parable of the Friend at Midnight does not appear to teach such things. In yet another sermon on the parable, however, Augustine omits almost all allegorical references and speaks of prayer only in the Lukan context mentioned above. Echoing the well-known rhetorical locus, "How much more," Augustine describes the parable as "a comparison by way of contrast." He follows the logic of Jesus, who exclaims, "If you then, who are evil, know how to give good gifts to your children, how much more will the heavenly Father give the Holy Spirit to those who ask for him!"

57

(Luke 11:13). He pastorally explains how asking for riches will not make us "good" and suggests that we ask instead for those gifts that are "good-making" (*Essential Sermons*, 166–71).

The theologian John Milbank claims that allegory and other figurative readings are necessary for the fullest rendering of the biblical text and for the creation of theology itself. He says historicist readings routinely separate what Augustine called "a sign" (Latin *signum*) in the text—its figures, stories, and characters—from the "thing" (*res*), an essential theological meaning held by the church catholic. In relation to the Old Testament, the modern loss of allegory, along with the polysemous character of Scripture in general, has resulted in the thinning of the christocentric nature of the word (*Word Made Strange*, 94–95). Eventually the church experienced an impoverishment of the text and its riches: we no longer enjoy an embarrassment *of* riches, but suffer a peculiarly modernist embarrassment *at* or *on account of* the riches offered by traditional biblical interpretation.

While I do not disagree with Milbank's conclusions, I do want to recognize that in the parables of Jesus, including the Friend at Midnight, a clear theological symbol, a "thing" (*res* = reality), is vitally present: the kingdom of God. Virtually all the parables live in the neighborhood of this theological symbol. Insisting that they must also yield instruction on the nature of the Trinity, the importance of the Scriptures, and other theological data transforms the parable into a combination lock. But if the parable is (merely) a code to be broken or a lock to be picked, it will not enrich the reader's understanding but divert attention from its main mission, which is to disclose the dawning reign of God and the crisis of the hearer's response.

Theory III: Parables Teach One Truth

When it comes to the interpretation of parables, there is no safety in numbers. If allegory breeds the multiplication of meanings in service to dogma, the modernist interpreter wishes to protect the integrity of the narrative (and the gospel) by insisting on the singularity of meaning. The modern antagonism to the multivalent reading of the parables began with Jülicher in the late nineteenth century. He reduced each parable to a single moral or spiritual principle, whose truth was capable of the widest possible application. The only way to understand a parable is to discover the one thing it means to say (or do), the *tertium* ("third thing" that connects the abstract theological idea with a vivid picture), and to disregard its peripheral or alleged allegorical elements.

There are reasons why we are drawn to the singularity of meaning; but before we test the theory against one or two parables, we need to understand our attraction to the single-point theory of interpretation. Theologically, the singularity of meaning contributes to the rational distillation of the church's teachings. We have already discussed how, in the hands of Dodd and Jeremias, a universal moral of each parable gave way to the centrality of the kingdom of God and, in the case of Jeremias, a catalog of "a few simple essential ideas" drawn from salvation history. In the twentieth century allegorical reading was replaced by form and redaction criticism. Both methods sought the single purpose or the theological agenda of the text. Bultmann asked his key question of all the material in the New Testament: How does the literary character of a particular "unit" answer a question, further the program, or exemplify a concern of the primitive church? A healing or a saying may be rich in dramatic or literary nuance, but what is most interesting to the interpreter is its bottom line—the function delivered by its form—which may be as simple and broad as the confirmation of Jesus' divinity, the rejection of temple authority, or a defense of the mission to the Gentiles. Likewise, it is possible for redaction criticism, which seeks to uncover the evangelist's particular theological tendency, to overlook a story's literary character in favor of its focus on the theology of the Gospel in question. Thus the Lukan version of the parable of the Great Feast, discussed above, is assigned a singular meaning based on the editorial choices Luke has made in order to sharpen his own theological interests. In this way, a highly complex narrative can be boiled down to one essential meaning. All this is to say that we have higher critical reasons for warming to the single-point theory of interpretation.

The New Testament, moreover, itself is a single-minded rhetorical document. Every one of Jesus' miracles or pronouncements participates in an arrow-like movement toward the crucifixion and resurrection of the Son of God. The forward-looking Gospel of Mark, for example, actually represents a reading *back* of all the Jesus stories in light of this transformative hope. When, for example,

59

Jesus stills a storm, casts out demons, or raises someone from the dead, these events act as a compass, always pointing in the same direction toward his lordship of creation, triumph over Satan, and his own victory over death. All four Gospels are about one thing.

The church's official calendar and lectionary are similarly organized to lead the people of God to a single conclusion. The readings from the Revised Common Lectionary, for example, are not organized around historical or chronological concerns; they are driven by the theological goal to elicit a single confession from the reader: "He is risen. He is risen indeed!" The lessons leading up to Easter do not skip from topic to topic but discipline us to keep our eyes on the prize. Following Easter, the appointed readings in the Gospels and Acts do not move on to other things but show us what it means to have a risen Teacher until, weeks later at Pentecost, we witness the full realization of his power. Given these biblical and liturgical realities, how could the interpreter *not* be open to a single-meaning theory of the parables?

Rhetorical and homiletical methods also play a part in the single-point theory. When I teach the introductory course in preaching, I require my students to identify the unifying idea or the core concern of the text. Although I remind them that their articulation of this "one thing" must unify the *whole* text (and not rely on a phrase or a single verse) and convey some dimension of the gospel, the assignment remains: students are to seek the single, unifying center of the text. No doubt this homiletical approach is born of the biblical and liturgical concerns outlined in the above paragraphs; yet even in their absence, from a rhetorical point of view everyone knows that an unfocused, multifaceted sermon is a disaster. How many points should a good sermon have? At least one. Once upon a time, Sunday dinner (of roast preacher) was devoted to a conversation about the morning's sermon. "What was the sermon about?" was the question. "Well, he talked about a lot of things." End of conversation.

For centuries, homiletics' closest ally was not biblical studies or liturgics, but rhetoric. In the United States, the majority of masters' and doctoral dissertations on preaching have been produced in departments of rhetoric and speech-communications. Even if today's homiletician does not accept "persuasion" as a sufficient description of the sermon's rhetorical aims (as I emphatically do not), one cannot overlook rhetoric's perennial concern with persuasion, which is the use of every trick in the book to induce the

60

hearer to do the speaker's bidding. A massive communications and advertising industry has refined the ancient art to a lucrative science. Moreover, the persuaders and the persuadees appear to have formed a symbiotic partnership. We have been groomed to crave the bite-sized information our media feeds us. For example, the whole notion of the *takeaway*, as in "What is the takeaway on global warming?" Or "What is the takeaway on the Middle East or Afghanistan?"—so typical of our culture's aversion to reasoned discussion—ultimately creates an atmosphere in which a single-truth theory of interpretation is the only viable one.

Thus for a variety of reasons, some valid and some decidedly not, the purpose-built sermon continues to seek the "one thing . . . needful" (Luke 10:42 KJV).

And at some level, each parable *is* about one solid thing. But finding the takeaway is not always easy, and in many cases it is impossible. For example, take the similitude of the Treasure in the Field in Matthew 13:44: "The kingdom of heaven is like treasure hidden in a field, which someone found and hid; then in his joy he goes and sells all that he has and buys that field." At first glance, of course, the kingdom is like hidden treasure. That little comparison makes sense; the kingdom is of surpassing value and, like a lot of valuable things, it lies hidden from our ordinary experience. But the nominative "kingdom" quickly gives way to a colorless actor, an indefinite "someone," whose subsequent action is as morally gray as his identity. He is not even a "certain man," only a "someone" (*anthrōpos*, "a person"). The nouns and pronouns quickly turn into the past-tense verbs "found" and "hid," suggesting a major discrepancy between parable time and real time. Finally, after a period of unspecified duration, he "goes and sells" (back to the present tense) "all that he has" in order to take possession of the field and the treasure he hid in it long ago. Oh yes, and one more thing: he acquires the field and its treasure, not out of Gekko-like greed or by means of moral subterfuge, but with great joy.

Now, what is *the* point? We ponder the possibilities:

1. The kingdom is of surpassing value.
2. The kingdom is a reality hidden from our experience, but we can find it.
3. The kingdom requires the sacrifice of all that we have.
4. The kingdom is pure joy.

How is the interpreter or preacher to isolate one truth in this deceptively simple little story? The answer is that the entire complex is brief and compact enough to be read as a singular entity encompassing both nouns of identity and verbs of action. Especially verbs, five of them in the space of one sentence: *found, hid, goes, sells, buys*. The kingdom is not a thing after all, but a verb, and it can be entered into only through some approximation of those five verbs. Perhaps it would be clearer if the parable began not with "The kingdom of heaven is like . . . ," which misleads the reader by indicating that we will be listing the attributes of something called "kingdom," but with "The kingdom of heaven is as if . . ." (cf. Mark 4:26). But most of Jesus' parables either begin with no formula of comparison or one in which a noun-to-noun comparison is made—the kingdom is like a man, a seed, some yeast—out of which verbs sprout and around which actions occur. (Only in Luke do Jesus' parables begin with normal conversational interactions, such as "What do you think?" or "Suppose one of you . . .").

I can tell you from my experience as a teacher that the main "point" addressed by most students is not found in the above list. In dealing with Matthew 13:44, most are preoccupied with a modern concern, and that is the apparent duplicity of the person who hides the treasure in order to acquire it for himself. We have laws against that sort of maneuver. For Matthew, however, the truest commentary on the man's apparent "duplicity" is not our moral qualms about his behavior, but the Lord's command to sell everything and "follow me" (19:21). The action of *hiding* is mysteriously important, as it is in the parable of the Yeast in Matthew 13:33, where the NRSV inexplicably translates "hid" (Greek, RSV) as "mixed in with," but it is not ethically significant to the evangelist. Too many sermons on this parable, however, get lost in moral casuistry and justifications of what appears to be questionable behavior, and never quite get to the joy of finding.

The tradition unanimously "solves" the interpretation of the parable by ignoring Jesus' phrase "the kingdom of heaven" and focusing attention on the meaning of the "treasure." In most cases the treasure either stands for an individual virtue, such as virginity, wisdom, or voluntary poverty—or a theological value, such as the Bible or the two natures of Christ (Wailes, *Medieval Allegories*, 118–20).

What does the parable mean? How can a single sentence be so difficult?

Not long ago I came across a young pastor's sermon on this text in which the preacher makes an interpretive move that no one in the tradition seems to have considered. He writes, "When Jesus was taken from the cross, they hid his body in a tomb and then sealed it lest someone find him. For three days, Jesus himself was the Treasure hidden in the field; for three days he was the seed lying dormant in the ground. . . . He was a human parable of God's love and power." It is fair to say that neither Jesus nor the author of Matthew's Gospel intended that to be *the* meaning of the parable. Nevertheless, the preacher, who was not schooled in the church's rich tradition of theological interpretation, has managed to speak in perfect continuity with that tradition and, in the process, declare something "new." To suggest that Jesus is the Treasure hidden in the field is an allegory, but one that transcends the specific virtues or truths often associated with "the treasure." We might term the preacher's reading "theologically holistic" in its capture of the larger reality of the kingdom of God.

Here we approach a view of "meaning" that cannot be limited to authorial intent, neither Jesus' nor Matthew's, but encompasses the reality of something larger. The concept of meaning does not merely *designate* a set of understandings that obtained in first-century Palestine, for the parables also *generate* a more comprehensive meaning and project it into the future. Where does that meaning come from? It emerges from the new situation, the new community created and reshaped by Jesus' ministry of storytelling and by his death and resurrection. Because of all that he accomplished, he now inhabits his own speech, and his language transcends the concept of kingdom and all its attributes. In that more capacious experience of meaning, the crucified one is the Treasure hidden in the field.

What we have said of the thirty-one-word (Greek) sentence in Matthew 13:44 is doubly true of the longer and more complex narrative parables, which are even less likely to yield a single truth. We have already discussed the difficulty in finding a center in the parable of the Wicked Tenants, an elliptically shaped story whose focus appears to shift from the owner's intention to the tenants' response and back again to the owner's final act of resolution. In this movement the most highly valued character in the story, the son, takes only a passive role.

63

Many parables resist the one-point theory. When Helmut Thielicke preached on the Prodigal Son, he found its thrust so divided that he preached two sermons on it, one for each of the two brothers. The preacher may follow the same procedure for Matthew's allegory of the Great Feast, which includes a second movement, the parable of the Improper Garment.

To sum it up in a single point (with three clauses!): A parable may indeed teach one truth, but you will need to dig for it, and when you find it, it will be more than you bargained for.

Theory IV: Parables Undermine "the Truth"

The parables of Jesus operate against a background of Israel's sacred history, values, and personages that, taken together, constitute its mythos, its grand and internalized account of itself. The myth includes the chosenness of Israel, the rectitude of divine judgment, the purity of religious observance, the glory of power, the righteousness of the law, and the separateness of a people. These are the pillars of Israel's universe; they contribute in great measure to the Christian mythos as well. Myths are not necessarily fanciful, made-up stories from long ago; they are the massive structures upon which a civilization or religion is built and by which it reconciles the inherent contradictions in its own past. For example, in the United States, the originating quest for freedom must somehow coexist with the original sin of slavery. A people chosen by God sins grievously against God. That contradiction can only be reconciled by the sacrifices of the Civil War and the death of Lincoln, from which comes another "original" American idea: the brotherhood of all. Myths undergird the unity of a people, but they also falsify the truth and lead a civilization to misconstrue its own character, destiny, and purpose in the world. For example, from the dialectics of the American myth of freedom comes the mission to impose a particular form of freedom on other nations.

In his early work on the parables, John Dominic Crossan associates the myth-busting work of the gospel with the genre of parable. To be a true parable, according to Crossan, a saying or story must *undermine* the dominant myth. Only parable can undermine big truths, for only in the brief moment of awareness created by what Crossan calls the "breaks of language," that is, in poetry or parabolic language, is it possible to make an accurate assessment of our existence. We come to our truest selves when we seek to act and speak in the crisis moment. Crossan's notion of parable roughly corresponds to Virginia Woolf's "lucid moments," James Joyce's "epiphanies," Kierkegaard's "fragments versus Christendom," and even Bonhoeffer's "hidden discipline." Like the parables of Jesus, these heightened moments of awareness open small windows onto the mystery of God's presence in the world. In the moment of disclosure, our pretentions to righteousness are laid bare, and our utter dependence on God is clarified. In Crossan's view, parable *always* suggests a particular kind of critique, an undermining, but it does so indirectly and even backhandedly. We crave a belly laugh, but parable smirks. We need the affirming hug, but parable only winks. We demand, "Thus says the Lord," but parable replies, "Perhaps." "They [parables] are stories which shatter the deep structure of our accepted world and thereby render clear and evident to us the relativity of story itself. They remove our defenses and make us vulnerable to God. It is only in such experiences that God can touch us, and only in such moments does the kingdom of God arrive" (Crossan, *Dark Interval*, 122; cf. 47–62).

One of Crossan's examples is Mark 4:30–32, the parable of the Mustard Seed. The mustard seed was legendary for its small size. The kingdom of God is like a mustard seed, which is the smallest of all the seeds on earth; but when it is grown up, it is the greatest of shrubs with branches so large that birds can make nests in its shade (*Dark Interval*, 93–96).

In my terminology, we can read this parable *straight* or *crooked*. The straight reading focuses on the contrast between tiny origins and larger endings. In Luke 17:6 Jesus refers to faith as a "grain of mustard seed" (RSV) that is able to toss a mulberry tree into the sea. That's the way the kingdom is, a humble, hidden presence on earth, in marked contrast to its anticipated glory at the last day. The placement of the parable in Mark constitutes an unmistakable reference to the beginning of Jesus' ministry, in what the writer C. P. Snow called the "time of hope," when in a young man's life anything and everything is still possible. "Beloved," says John the apostle, "it does not yet appear what we shall be" (1 John 3:2 RSV). When Paul wished to contrast the earthly body with its resurrected state, he too drew from the imagery of seeds and wheat: "What is sown is perishable, what is raised is imperishable. It is sown in dishonor, it is raised in glory. It is sown in weakness, it is raised in power" (1 Cor. 15:42–44). This is a comforting reading, not

65

comfortable, but a reading capable of bringing a sense of assurance and hope to individuals who face death or to communities that are enduring loss or persecution. I know people who are living illustrations of the straight reading of this parable: a man who has devoted his entire working life to helping homeless people, a couple who gave thirty years of their lives in an Indian village, a doctor who has devoted her career to the plight of children with preventable diseases. When I read about the Mustard Seed, I think of them and others like them, working in relative anonymity and with no expectation of a reward, but whose faithfulness, according to Mark 4:32, will leaf out in blessings unimaginable.

The *crooked* reading is more speculative but quite intriguing from a literary point of view. It too is a comforting reading, but its comfort comes with sharper edges and fewer "handles." Crossan's point is simple. What is Jesus implying about the kingdom of God when he compares it to a "shrub"? Why would he use a mustard shrub as a symbol of the kingdom when he had the cedars of Lebanon at his homiletic disposal? In Ezekiel 31 God announces the demise of Egypt by comparing it to one of the cedars of Lebanon, with its mighty branches and great height:

> So it towered high above all the trees of the field;
> Its boughs grew large and its branches long,
>   from abundant water in its shoots.
> All the birds of the air made nests in its boughs.
>   (Ezek. 31:5–6)

A similar figure appears in Daniel 4. In both places the tree signifies a great empire waiting to be cut down to size by Israel's God. With the word "shrub," Jesus presumably is refusing to clothe his kingdom in the grandiosity of ancient empires. It is not that sort of kingdom. It lies hidden in ordinary acts of obedience and extraordinary gestures of love. But beyond these general observations on the scaled-back nature of the kingdom of God, Crossan doesn't identify the target of Jesus' gentle satire, nor does he explain how it would have been received by the earliest community. Did its first hearers "get it"? To dramatize the kingdom as "subversive" on the basis of this parable seems a bit grandiose itself.

66   We have no indication from Mark 4 that anyone got the shrub joke. In a chapter in which Jesus has already decoded the parable of the Sower, the evangelist has a perfect opportunity to explain

the difference between the expected tree and a lowly shrub. But he does not. If anyone understood the joke, it was Luke, who in his version of the parable replaces "shrub" with "tree" (13:19). He either caught on to what Mark was doing and didn't like it, or he didn't get the joke and therefore felt compelled to "fix" the script by heightening the contrast between the mustard seed and its final product. Matthew has it both ways by rendering Mark's shrub as "the greatest of shrubs and becomes a tree" (Matt. 13:32).

The straight reading of the parable is the obvious reading, and it delivers a powerful and comforting message of the kingdom of God. What I have termed the crooked reading is far more speculative. It posits a sophisticated literary sensibility on the part of Mark, one that passes for genuine cleverness, but whose immediate theological payoff remains slight. In other words, why go to all that literary trouble simply for the sake of toying with the reader's expectations?

It is not until the next episode in the chapter, the Storm on the Lake, that we begin to get the hang of this new, human-scaled kingdom. It happens when we see a new, human-scaled Son of God caught in what W. H. Auden terms "the human position," that is, a position of utter vulnerability. Mark frames the scene like a cinematographer; he creates an effect so stunningly visual that the reader has no difficulty "seeing" what he wants us to see. A flotilla of boats sets out from the shore, but soon the other boats disappear from the scene, and the camera zooms in on one boat in particular, and then on one person in that boat. It is the Messiah, sound asleep in the stern, curled up in the fetal position on "the cushion." If Crossan is right about the shrub joke, then we are faced with yet another amazing realignment of the mythic expectations. Psalm 121:4 offers the ultimate picture of divine protection in the figure of an unsleeping God. "He who keeps Israel will neither slumber nor sleep." Like the difference between a cedar tree and a mustard shrub, the contrast between the unsleeping God and "the Son of God" (Mark 1:1) asleep in the storm is stunning. What does it mean? Where will it all lead?

Crossan says it leads to a completely new understanding of how God is present to us in the world. It leads to the cross. And here, despite his somewhat undeveloped and unconvincing theory of the Mustard Seed, Crossan's theory turns to theology and begins to make sense. The Messiah finally quits telling parables— Crossan (and Jeremias) claims the church turned them all into

67

allegories—and the crucified one himself becomes the Parable of God (*Dark Interval*, 123–26). Humble, hidden, kenotic, ironic, and subversive—in Jesus, God undermines the most evil empire of all, the kingdom of death, and brings life to light by a most unlikely means.

Parable undermines "the truth" in order to liberate the Truth.

CHAPTER 3

Reading the Parables with Mark, Matthew, and Luke

For the purpose of teaching and preaching the parables in a religious assembly, which is the near-universal context of their interpretation, one can find no better guide than the Synoptic evangelists. In this chapter we will read *with* the evangelists and learn from their interpretations. We do so for two reasons: the evangelists' interpretive presentations of the parables have the authority of the church's canon, or "rule," by which all other literature that purports to render the truth of Jesus Christ is measured. By mentioning "the church," I do not mean to suggest a top-down regimen of interpretation, but the gathered practices of countless Christians who read the Scripture together in their various communities. By reading *with* the evangelists, we are reading with the church and seeking its elusive unity, not as an institutional entity, but as a reading body that acknowledges the authority of a common Scripture.

When we notice the obviously discrepant treatments of the received tradition—in this case, the parables—we are acknowledging that the evangelists were in their own way teachers, preachers, and pastors to their respective communities. By honoring their interpretations and respectfully discriminating among them, we are linking our efforts on behalf of our respective communities with theirs of another age. For example, when we recognize that Luke has appended three separate explanations to the parable of

69

the Dishonest Steward, we can assume that the evangelist did not create the story but received it, and that he was as puzzled by it as we are. Where redactional efforts are obvious, as they are in Luke 16, the modern interpreter is invited to search for an earlier written or oral version of the parable. Such a procedure may lead to interesting theories about the development of the parable and the nature of the community or communities that received it, but it will not produce anything approaching historical verification. For if we have learned anything from Jeremias and the many others who have investigated the sources of the parables, it is that, aside from a few methodological rules for distinguishing earlier from later material, the results are almost always speculative and open to enormous disagreement within the community of parable scholarship.

The second reason for reading with the evangelists is historical: despite our sophisticated methods of analysis, Mark, Matthew, and Luke (whoever they were) knew more about Jesus and his parables than we do. I understand that this claim is not obvious to everyone. The great historian Leopold von Ranke said, "Every age is equidistant to eternity," which is true enough in the sense that God does not favor the wisdom of one era above another. Some would supplement von Ranke's claim by adding, "Every age is equidistant to Jesus," which is also true in terms of the life of faith and prayer. But when it comes to history and historical research, where facts and chronology still count for something, the Synoptic evangelists "knew people who knew people." Even if they were not eyewitnesses, they lived within a generation of the originating events of the New Testament. Luke's statement of his historical method is worth quoting in full:

> Since many have undertaken to set down an orderly account of the events that have been fulfilled among us, just as they were handed on to us by those who from the beginning were eyewitnesses and servants of the word, I too decided, after investigating everything carefully from the very first, to write an orderly account for you. . . .
>
> (Luke 1:1–3)

The peculiar genius of Christianity, or one of the many manifestations of that genius, is that its confession of faith ("I believe") is punctuated by historical data ("crucified under Pontius Pilate"),

70

which means that the chain of historical testimony and the practice of historical reasoning will always be a part of Christian theology and biblical scholarship.

A great deal has been written about the transmission of the Jesus tradition and the interrelations of the Synoptic Gospels. So much, in fact, that I am freed to make introductory comments in the broadest possible strokes. In that vein, let us briefly review what might be called the "Parabolic Problem." Each of the Synoptic Gospels presupposes the existence of an *author* ("Mark," "Matthew," and "Luke") who, unlike the evangelist John, "disappears" into an unnamed and unobtrusive *narrator* of the Gospel. If not omniscient in a literary sense, the narrators in Mark, Matthew, and Luke control the entire story of Jesus' earthly ministry, death, and resurrection. Within the scope of that responsibility, all three narrate an account of Jesus telling parables. Thus whenever we read the parables, we are encountering a limited narrator (= Jesus, a character in the story), who is "controlled" by a more comprehensive narrator (= the evangelist). The character is telling a series of little stories, which are lodged within a larger and more all-encompassing story. The smaller stories—the parables—are generally compatible with the style and theological aims of the larger story, the Gospels in their entirety. In the three Gospels' account of the parables, then, we encounter what literary critics call "an imitation of a narrator telling a story" (Scholes and Kellogg, *Nature of Narrative*, 54). In this "imitation" the three authors/narrators obscure their own narrative voice and—by means of description, plot, dialogue, and characterization—allow the small stories to express their theological convictions, which are presumably consistent with Jesus' message.

The interpretive problem intensifies when the two narratives differ, that is, when the evangelist's "reading" of one of the little stories appears to be at odds with Jesus' telling of it, or when the evangelist's technique obviously shapes the manner in which Jesus' story is reported, or when the evangelists' accounts of the parable do not agree with one another. Sometimes the characters in a parable betray knowledge of the whole Gospel, for example, in the parable of Lazarus and the Rich Man, when Abraham says that the brothers will not believe "even if someone rises from the dead" (Luke 16:31). In these cases there is seepage between the smaller

71

and larger stories and a confusion of two separate audiences. This produces irony, which is broadly defined as a significant discrepancy between what is said or written and how it is heard or read by a more informed audience.

Before we begin reading with the evangelists, let us take a step back from these complicated matters and remind ourselves of the distinct theological agendas at work among the Synoptic Gospels. What follows are three versions of the same tradition:

Mark 8:11–12. The Pharisees came and began to argue with him, asking him for a sign from heaven, to test him. And he sighed deeply in his spirit and said, "Why does this generation ask for a sign? Truly I tell you, no sign will be given to this generation." And he left them, and getting into the boat again, he went across to the other side.

Luke 11:29–32. When the crowds were increasing, he began to say, "This generation is an evil generation; it asks for a sign, but no sign will be given to it except the sign of Jonah. For just as Jonah became a sign to the people of Nineveh, so the Son of Man will be to this generation. The queen of the South will rise at the judgment with the people of this generation and condemn them, because she came from the ends of the earth to listen to the wisdom of Solomon, and see, something greater than Solomon is here! The people of Nineveh will rise up at the judgment with this generation and condemn it, because they repented at the proclamation of Jonah, and see, something greater than Jonah is here!"

Matthew 12:38–42. Then some of the scribes and Pharisees said to him, "Teacher, we wish to see a sign from you." But he answered them, "An evil and adulterous generation asks for a sign, but no sign will be given to it except the sign of the prophet Jonah. For just as Jonah was three days and three nights in the belly of the sea monster, so for three days and three nights the Son of Man will be in the heart of the earth. The people of Nineveh will rise up at the judgment with this generation and condemn it, because they repented at the proclamation of Jonah, and see, something greater than Jonah is here! The queen of the South will rise up at the judgment with this generation and condemn it, because she came from the ends of the earth to listen to the wisdom of Solomon, and see, something greater than Solomon is here!"

72   In Mark, Jesus issues no explicit condemnation of the Pharisees or the present generation. He simply sighs and refuses to give a sign. Then he leaves. The passage contains no figurative or indirect

language. Mark sandwiches the episode between two boating episodes in which Jesus speaks of bread with his disciples. By his placement of the passage, Mark may be implying that the feeding of the four thousand *is* just the sign they are asking for, but the Pharisees are incapable of recognizing it.

Both Luke and Matthew introduce the phrase "Son of Man," to whom Jesus refers exclusively in the third person. In both evangelists the saying is extended into two similes or simile-like comparisons. The comparison of Jesus with Jonah in Luke and Matthew is reminiscent of rabbinic comment and would in other places qualify as a "parable." Both evangelists interweave an allusion to the queen of the South, who traveled a great distance to admire the wisdom of Solomon. Her inclusion serves as a judgment on the current generation's failure to perceive "something greater than Solomon" in its midst.

The comparison of the Son of Man (Jesus) and Jonah in the two Gospels, however, takes two, very different directions. In each of the two Gospels, Jonah functions as a sign. In Luke, it is Jonah's preaching: just as Jonah preached repentance to the people of Nineveh, so the Son of Man will do in this generation.

In Matthew the pivotal sign is Jonah's burial in the sea monster and then resurrection, which Matthew allegorizes by reference to Jesus' three days and nights "in the heart of the earth." Thus what begins as a simple refusal to give a sign in the Gospel of Mark, in Luke's Gospel becomes the sign of Jonah's preaching, and finally, by the addition of a single sentence in the Gospel of Matthew, is transformed into an allegory of death, burial, and resurrection.

To summarize: Mark's Gospel is *eschatological*, with its emphasis falling on the decisive deeds of Jesus, the Son of God. His ministry represents the act of God's breaking into history to bind the strong man and to inaugurate the reign of God (3:23–27). In Mark, events will unfold quickly toward the crucifixion and resurrection of Jesus, too quickly to allow for extensive teaching and storytelling on the part of God's Messiah. The relative absence of parables in Mark—he has only six—colors the shape and tone of the entire Gospel. Jesus' sudden appearance in Galilee reads like the perfect illustration of Dodd's "realized eschatology." In the person of Jesus, God is stepping onto the highway of history. "Prepare the way of the Lord, make his paths straight." In Mark, the Great Harvest eschatology of chapter 4 eventually disappears from view, to

73

be replaced by the Cosmic Appearing depicted in the Little Apocalypse in chapter 13, whose date of occurrence is known to no one but the Father.

If Mark is eschatological, Matthew is *ecclesiological* and *didactic*. Where Mark hurries toward catastrophe, Matthew tarries long enough to organize his Gospel into a series of lessons, many of which are buttressed by allegorical parables such as the Wicked Tenants in chapter 21, the Wedding Banquet in chapter 22, and the Ten Bridesmaids and the Judgment of the Nations in chapter 25.

Based on the Jonah comparisons noted above, one might have expected this chapter to culminate with comments on Matthew's ecclesiology and allegorical parables, since in many ways his Gospel appears to represent the greatest density and most carefully developed version of the Jesus story. However, the flow of the parables appears to move in another direction. The Gospel of Luke is less preoccupied with ecclesial and intramural conflicts with Judaism than is Matthew and is more *missional* and *literary* in character. In Luke the parables are meant to carry the reader away from the scenes of Jesus' ministry and into the book of Acts. In his Gospel the story of Jesus' ministry *ends* with an ascension; in the book of Acts the mission of the church *begins* with an ascension. From a literary point of view, the earthbound ministry of Jesus concludes in the only way it can. From a theological perspective, the universal expansion of the church is made possible not by Jesus' disappearance but his universal lordship as symbolized by his ascension. He now sits at the right hand of the Father, which, as Luther said, means "everywhere." Jesus is now free to be everywhere.

In the Gospel of Luke the parables assume a literary identity appropriate to the universal status of their teller and the universalizing tendency of the church. Of the three Synoptic Gospels, Luke is most concerned to craft the parables in such a way that they comport with the literatures of his era. In the artistry of their characterization, setting, and dialogue, his parables of the Unjust Judge, the Dishonest Steward, the Prodigal Son, the Good Samaritan, the Pharisee and the Tax Collector, and several others participate in the literary conventions of his and every age. As Luke has drawn them, they open onto world literature, the expanding history of the movement, and the universals of human life.

The Gospel of Mark

In his "time of hope," Jesus compares the reign of God to the inevitability of natural growth. The sower throws caution to the winds and sows his seed profligately. The seed that falls into good soil produces an extraordinary return, yielding thirtyfold, sixtyfold, and a hundredfold. What is more miraculous than the return is that the sower takes no extraordinary steps or follows no special procedures to make it happen (Mark 4:1–9). He only sows. In the narrative proper, the word "mystery" does not occur. That is because in reference to the parable itself, nothing is hidden or secret. The same principle of growth is at work in the parable of the Mustard Seed (Mark 4:30–32). Whether it grows into a shrub or a tree does not matter. What counts is the explosion of growth in the kingdom of God.

The purest and most exuberant articulation of the good news of God's reign is found in the parable of the Growing Seed found in Mark 4:26–29:

> He also said, "The kingdom of God is as if someone would scatter seed on the ground, and would sleep and rise night and day, and the seed would sprout and grow, he does not know how. The earth produces of itself [Greek *automatē*], first the stalk, then the head, then the full grain in the head. But when the grain is ripe, at once he goes in with his sickle, because harvest has come."

In this parable, the kingdom is a verb. It is not a man or a seed or any *thing* at all, but an action: scatter, sprout, grow, produce. The one who scatters is favored with no hint of divine identity; he is not a rich farmer, an owner, or a manager. He possesses no special knowledge of soil types or any other expertise; he is an undetermined "someone." As if to underscore his lack of agricultural expertise, all he does after scattering (note the difference from "planting") is go to sleep at night and get up in the morning. The seed grows, but he doesn't have a clue how it happens. The earth takes over and of its own nature produces full grain in the head. Some have suggested that the portrait of automatic growth may be directed against revolutionary elements that want to "force the end" by military efforts against Rome (see Marcus, 326; and the discussion of the social context in chap. 5 below).

75

Although the account of the harvest is introduced by the word "but," that conjunction does not suggest conflict, sabotage, or punishment (as in Matthew's parable of the Wheat among the Weeds in 13:24–40, esp. v. 25). No portion of the harvest is thrown into the fire. The time of growth is over, the harvest has come. Harvest is the final phase in the cycle of growth, and as such it is appropriately greeted with joy and thanksgiving. "Come ye thankful people, come, / Raise the song of harvest home."

Despite the placidity of the Growing Seed, we continue to think of Mark's Gospel in eschatological terms. Why? Because the symmetry of nature will be polluted by evil, and the ministry of Jesus will be marred by conflict. The natural processes of the kingdom, suggested by the metaphor of untrammeled growth, will be interrupted by battles that end in apparent defeat. The growing fields will turn into killing fields. And yet, even in an eschatological Gospel in which Jesus' enemies, neighbors, and Beelzebub himself will come roaring after him, the parable of the Growing Seed breathes none of that rancid spirit. It remains an island of hope.

Still, no one can miss the intimations of conflict and failure already present in Mark 4. The narrative core of the parable of the Sower speaks of birds, thorns, and rocky soil. It announces that for whatever reason, some yields will exceed others. Jesus' "time of hope" in the early part of Mark's narrative is eclipsed by the parables themselves. They are mottled by shadows and are more than capable of creating darkness at every turn. Moreover, since the mystery of what is about to happen to Jesus is so deep and perverse, God must have had a hand in it from the beginning (Mark 4:10–12, see comments in chap. 2 above). Unsurprisingly, Jesus' explanation of the parable of the Sower turns into a catalog of failures caused by a variety of impediments (compare, for example, the "lure of wealth" in Mark 4:19 with the story of the rich young ruler in 10:17–22).

Mark 4 represents either a sloppy editing job by the evangelist, or something deeper and more pervasive in the Jesus story. Mark 4 is either a mishmash of optimism, realism, and the darkest possible pessimism, or it is a skillful foreshadowing of the parabola of Jesus' ministry, death, and resurrection. If it is the latter, as I believe it is, the parables of chapter 4 also mirror the believer's life in the kingdom, in which hope, joy, abundance, and loss coexist with no logic other than the logic of Jesus' own story.

If the parable of the Growing Seed in Mark 4 illustrates the way God's reign was meant to be, the parable of the Wicked Tenants in chapter 12 tells what it has become. Both parables are set in places of growth. In one, the natural processes unfold in open spaces to a successful harvest. The other occurs in an artificially enclosed area, and the place of growth has become a fortress surrounded by a fence and protected by a watchtower. Strangers who themselves have no organic connection to the land have been put in charge of it. The owner, identified only as "a man," upgraded in Matthew to "the landowner," leases his property to tenants and then goes into another country. The vineyard produces, but not as the result of a natural or miraculous process that would lead to abundance. It is under new and ominous management.

The open-ended parable of the automatically Growing Seed has become an allegory of spoilage and vindictiveness in the vineyard. Point for point, the parable of the Wicked Tenants rehearses Israel's history of rebellion, which climaxes in the murder of the son, the "heir" and therefore the true owner of the vineyard, whose body is thrown outside the wall, an echo of which is heard in Hebrews 13:12: "Therefore Jesus also suffered outside the city gate in order to sanctify the people by his own blood."

The death of the son marks the end of the story. The many threats against Jesus and the controversies surrounding his ministry are summed up in the final verse of the narrative proper: "And they took him and killed him" (Mark 12:8 RSV). All the rest is commentary. The entire Synoptic tradition uses Jesus' commentary as justification of God's wrath on those who mistreated the son and God's favor bestowed on "others." All three Gospels preserve the mixed metaphor of vineyard and building, though Luke complicates the already-confused image with two further additions: the cornerstone becomes an instrument of punishment: when it falls on someone, it will crush him! (Luke 20:18). Mark's less contrived version of the parable represents not only the history of Israel's rejection of the servants of God, including Jesus; it also signals an ominous turn in the fortunes of the reign of God on earth.

Mark has no time for further teaching or ruminations on the ethics of the kingdom. The future is bearing down on Jesus. The magnificent harvest has been transferred to the future, when "not one stone will be left here upon another," and "all will be thrown down" (Mark 13:2). When Jesus prophesies false messiahs and

77

political persecution, he freely refers to himself: "Many will come in my name" (13:6). The disciples will be brought before governors and kings, he says, "because of me" (v. 9). But when the prophecy turns to apocalypse proper, and the sun grows dark and the stars fall from the sky, then the gentle teller of parables turns once again to his alter ego, the Son of Man (see comments in chap. 1 above). With fearful symmetry, the joyful harvest predicted in the parables of Mark 4 has been transformed into a cosmic harvest in which the Son of Man will gather the elect from the four winds and the ends of the earth (13:27). The eschatology of God's sudden appearance in Galilee has been replaced by an equally surprising eschatology of the Son of Man's appearance in the starless heavens.

For the time being, then, the only sort of kingdom parables that make sense in Mark's framework are parables of hiddenness. The kingdom of God has transcended itself—or collapsed into itself like heavy matter. The only way to find it now is to watch for signs. Just as the leafing of the fig tree teaches us that summer is near, so those who can read the clues of history will know that the Son of Man is approaching the gates (Mark 13:28–31).

No one knows when the end will come, not the angels in heaven, not even the Son, but only the Father (Mark 13:32). This is Jesus speaking once again, not the powerful Son of Man, whose cosmic power is so great that Jesus (or his community) cannot make an explicit identification of the two. Not knowing the day or the hour puts the community on high alert. The only thing believers know for sure is that it can happen anytime—and it will be sudden. When a man goes on a journey, he commands the doorkeeper to be on watch. What the master says to his slave, Jesus says to Mark's community and to ours: "Keep awake" (13:32–37).

For further details, see Matthew.

The Gospel of Matthew

The urgency of Mark's use of parable takes another form in the Gospel of Matthew. The "time of hope" that seemed so appropriately placed near the beginning of Mark's Gospel has been scaled back and placed in the third of the five great discourses into which Matthew has divided his Gospel. Like Mark, Matthew makes little effort to compose a narrative framework for his parables in chapter 13.

78

They come one after the other, several with no introduction and no attempt at contextualization. It is as if the evangelist is saying, "This is the tradition that I received. Here it is." The parable of the Sower is still there, amended and perhaps softened, as we have noted in the previous chapter, but the parable of the automatically Growing Seed has been replaced by intimations of evil in the wheat field.

In the parable of the Weeds among the Wheat (Matt. 13:24–30), Matthew tackles two vexing questions: How do wicked people gain entrance to the "field"? How shall the righteous deal with them? In the parable proper, the field is the kingdom of God (heaven), into which an "enemy" has sown "darnel," a common weed (13:24). That everyone was sleeping while it was sown is Matthew's warning to the saints: "Keep awake!" This parable is one of the few to approach the ancient philosophical dilemma, the question of the origin of evil, the question of *whence*. The slaves cannot understand how weeds could spring forth from a field in which "good" seed has been sown.

The householder replies by adding another actor to the cast: "an enemy has done this" (13:28). Apparently, this is explanation enough for the slaves. The implication of his reply is that even Matthew's church is not immune to the incursions of the enemy. Who exactly is the "enemy"? A shadowy figure, an Evil One, with powers capable of spoiling the kingdom-community. Years ago *The Bad Seed* (film, 1956) explored the origins of evil in a sweet little girl with pigtails. It was not her acts of murder that made the film such a big hit, but murder in one so young and innocent. More recently, an article in our local newspaper bore this title: "Lee County tobacco farmer at a loss over poisoning of his plants." "Why," the farmer asked, "would someone take the trouble to break into his greenhouse and spray herbicide on nearly one million of his tiny plants?" Like Jesus' parable, the news story had two parts: Why would someone do this? What can I do to limit my damages?

The second part of the parable has to do with church discipline. Shall we identify the sinners in this church and throw them out? Let's see, where shall we begin? The landowner declines to do this not so much in forgiveness for the sinners as in concern for what a rabid policy of church discipline might do to the fledgling plants. Instead, he will wait until the harvest, which in this parable has taken on an unambiguously ominous coloring. Then the weeds can be safely divided from the wheat; the weeds can be burned, but the wheat is to be gathered into the owner's barn.

79

If ever there was a parable that needs no explanation, it is this one. Thus it comes as something of a surprise when six verses later Jesus explains the parable of the Weeds among the Wheat (13:37–43). The original parable is about the kingdom of heaven; its language and theological concerns are those of the primitive Christian community. They voice Matthew's perennial concerns over the makeup of those who live in the field. The parable presupposes an enclosed entity, more a hothouse than a field, in which it is possible to evaluate the moral worth of each of its members. The slaves are the prophets and community leaders who tend this community and claim responsibility for its purity. Jesus' explanation adds allegorical specification and breadth to the parable. What is local in the original—a community concern—has become universal, and the mention of eschatological judgment at the very end of the original parable is now the centerpiece of the explanation. The characters have been magnified to universal significance. He who sows is the eschatological Son of Man; the enemy is the devil; the field is no longer the kingdom or the early community, but the "world"; the reapers are no longer the slaves, that is, church leaders, but angels sent to collect the evildoers.

The same message, with the same furnace of fire, is repeated a few verses later in the parable of the Net (Matt. 13:47–50). The bad fish are separated from the good fish and thrown into the fire. This is a detail that appears to violate the principles of fishing. The ocean is certainly full of unappetizing creatures, but when they hook the odd pigfish or sting ray, most fishermen throw them back in the water and watch them swim off. In short, Matthew's Jesus has abandoned the eschatological hopefulness with which Mark begins his Gospel and has drawn the lines between those who belong in God's church, kingdom, or world, and those who do not.

Only in Matthew's Gospel does Jesus ask, "Have you understood all this?" and then proceeds to supply his enigmatic explanation (Matt. 13:51–53). The disciples answer like children, "Yes," which is surely a lie. He says, "Therefore every scribe who has been trained for the kingdom of heaven is like the master of a household who brings out of his treasure what is new and what is old." Then he leaves.

80   Perhaps Matthew has placed this question and his veiled explanation at this point in his Gospel because of its proximity to the parable of the Treasure in the Field (13:44), with which it

shares the catchword "treasure." What is interesting is his comparison of a disciple with a scribe. In Judaism the scribe was a
secondary figure, like a copyist or a secretary, but *not* like a master of a household, who in the parable of the Weeds among the
Wheat and in later parables is usually thought to represent God or
Jesus. The disciple is such a scribe who is trained not merely for
the traditions of the fathers, but also for the kingdom of heaven.
The scribe will preserve, or copy, all that is eternal in the law and
the righteousness of God, and in so doing will find the greatest
treasure of all. Some scholars believe the verse is Matthew's own
tagline.

Matthew is famous for his hyperbole. His outlandish expressions, like logs in the eye or fish thrown into the fire, give his Gospel
a cartoonish character, though I hasten to add, cartoons are not
bad! A cartoon-like story can be an effective teaching instrument.
The walls of the great cathedrals in Europe were once filled with
colorful cartoon-like illustrations from the Bible until time and oxi-
dization caused them to disappear. In Matthew 18 two important
pastoral concerns come together. One is the moral composition of
the new Jesus community, which Matthew hopes to be filled by
disciples with the diligence of scribes. His second concern is the
importance of forgiveness. And between them, these two—purity
and generosity—have an uneasy history. It's not always clear that
the evangelist's community has solved the relationship of the two
concerns. Contemporary churches, too, wishing to embody both
the rigor of discipleship *and* the generosity of forgiveness, struggle
with and sometimes fail at the same issue.

The community must avoid being a source of offense. What's
the point of bringing seekers and new believers into the church
if what they find there only causes them to doubt the fundamental message of the gospel? Anyone whose talk or behavior causes
one of these "little ones"—no longer literal children but appren-
tice disciples—to stumble in faith (and here comes the cartoon)
should have a millstone placed around the neck and be drowned
(18:6–7). If there is something about your own personal makeup,
some habitual behavior or besetting sin, something that causes you
to doubt your own fitness for the kingdom, you might think about
cutting off the offending part of your body (vv. 8–9). Does your eye
stray toward places or people where it doesn't belong? Tear it out
and throw it away. This is serious comedy, for it is Jesus' peculiar

81

way of reminding his followers that church discipline begins with self-discipline.

Ironically, this draconian advice is followed by one of the most comforting statements in the New Testament. These beloved "little ones" are not forgotten and, presumably, will never stumble again. For in heaven they are assigned guardians who perform their task more effectively than their morally lax shepherds on earth. Their "angels," their heavenly alter egos, perpetually behold the face of the Father. These little ones stand for Jesus himself (cf. Matt. 18:5). A careful reading of the parable of the Lost Sheep that follows reveals the shepherd's care not for any and all lost souls but, again, for the newest, weakest, greenest, and most vulnerable of those who seek the kingdom of God, the "little ones" (18:10–14)

The rest of chapter 18 continues the interaction between discipline and forgiveness. Jesus tells a story about a king who wishes to "settle accounts" with his slaves (vv. 23–35). What follows is not a feel-good story but a reckoning between the king and his slaves who owe him money. Although this parable is located in the "forgiveness chapter" of the Gospel, its real theme has more to do with the disciplining of relationships within the early community. The king orders that the first slave be sold along with "his wife and children and all his possessions," in order to satisfy the debt. But the king and the slave know the debt can never be repaid, even by the money earned from the sale of one family. The unfortunate man is so out of touch with reality that he promises, "I will pay you everything." Out of pity the king cancels the debt and has him released from prison. The king's forgiveness, however, is not duplicated in the one forgiven, who shows his true colors by throttling a fellow slave who owes him a pittance and having him thrown into debtors' prison.

This is a story about the moral dynamics of a community. Its imagery reflects the greatest socioeconomic problem facing the tenant-farming class of Jesus' day: the problem of massive debt owed to landowning elites (see chap. 5 below). Read in that light, the owner's decision to forgive the entire debt constitutes a social as well as a theological statement. Whatever its economic implications, the tale is played out before an audience (community) of slaves who witness both the king's forgiveness and the first slave's refusal to forgive. The parable pivots on that irony, a spiritual imbalance that must have vexed the early Christian community. What is portrayed is not merely a story of God's forgiveness wasted, or a tale of human fallibility, but a more decisive and tragic negation that if unchecked or undisciplined threatens the basis of the community itself.

Failure to forgive within the Christian community cannot be forgiven by God because when we refuse to forgive we cancel the identity of God. Without forgiveness, God disappears from the earth. Without forgiveness, all we can know of God is the very thing we dread about God. It is not surprising, then, that the consequence of the first slave's offense—torture without a foreseeable end—is greater than the judgment originally pronounced by the king.

Of the Synoptic writers, Matthew is most concerned with questions of law. Yet in Matthew's universe, those who have failed to live up to the law are ushered into the kingdom of heaven. The story of the Workers in the Vineyard oscillates between two familiar settings, the marketplace and the vineyard, the world and the kingdom (22:1–16). In this story the marketplace functions as the anteroom to the kingdom. The marketplace is a zone of hopelessness and idleness, where the unemployed have no opportunity of doing the work characteristic of the kingdom.

In T. S. Eliot's "Choruses from the Rock," the workers (the "humble") declare that they are willing to build "with new bricks" where "the beams are rotten," and with "new speech" where "the word is unspoken," but

> No man has hired us
> With pocketed hands
> And lowered faces
> We stand about in open places
> And shiver in unlit rooms.
> (*Selected Poems*, 110)

But the owner in the parable apparently has a heart for workers, which may explain his odd hiring practices. We see him hire at 9:00 a.m., at noon, at 3:00 p.m., and at 5:00. From all we can gather from this pattern, he may be out there now—outside the implied confines of the narrative—cruising the marketplace in search of men and women who need work.

Like the story of the Unforgiving Slave, the graciousness exhibited by the owner/king in this parable takes a more dramatic turn at the climax of the parable. This story, too, features a reckoning.

83

Once again, the theodrama depends on an audience, which is the community recognizing the grace that created the vineyard in the first place. The audience to this parable exists wherever communities are struggling to live by grace amid the world's alternative arrangements, where its members must sort through their many racial and economic differences and come to a mutual understanding of their respective places in the kingdom. When they do not, the contemporary community, like the assembly of workers at the end of the day, erupts in disappointment and resentment.

The primary audience to the owner's generosity is the workers who were hired first. They are the veterans of the vineyard, whose hard work and long tenure have created certain expectations of reward. They are weary, and their weariness is that of the righteous. The vineyard is *cosa nostra*, "our thing"; like the renters in the parable of the Wicked Tenants, they may even think they own the place. If the owner had paid them first and gotten them off the scene, trouble would have been avoided. Yet the point is not to avoid trouble but to teach the veterans a hard but valuable lesson. They *must* watch, or the parable will have no effect.

Many interpreters claim that the parable is unpalatable to modern readers because it violates contemporary labor practices and the standards of equal pay for equal work (see the continuing discussion in chap. 5 below). But as the reaction of those hired first demonstrates, the landowner's practices were as offensive in the first century as they are in the twenty-first. We have heard the accusation in bargaining sessions and seen the signs on the picket lines: UNFAIR. What is maddening about the story, however, is that the workers are *not* given unequal wages: they all get the same. What could be fairer than that? The question moves us to a prior consideration: Don't those who have worked the longest *deserve* the most? Who among us hasn't felt similar stirrings when the late arrival is upgraded to first class, or the lazy one is given an extension on work everyone else has completed?

The workers claim their just deserts on the basis of their hard work and length of service, in other words, on qualities related to *them* and their performance in the vineyard. The owner dismisses their argument out of hand because it ignores a quality *in him*, namely, his freedom to reward his workers as he sees fit. The owner replies in verse 15, "Is your eye evil because I am good?" (NRSV mg.). As it turns out, the entire basis of reward has nothing to do

84

with the qualities of the workers or their length of service. "It's not about you," the landowner might have said, "or about your pitiful need to replicate the notions of equality and inequality found in the marketplace. You do not belong to the marketplace anymore. No, it's all about me and my generosity." It is important for the veterans of the vineyard to witness this drama, to hear the owner's speech, and to understand it, for his generosity will form and define the basis of the communities in which they live. Like the essential importance of forgiveness in the Christian community (cf. Matt. 18), the generosity of God—call it "grace"—is equally nonnegotiable. You won't find it in the marketplace, but only in the vineyard of the Lord. In order to underscore the dramatic reversal of expectations, Matthew book-ends the parable with similar versions of the saying, "So the last will be first, and the first will be last" (20:16; cf. 19:30).

At the core of the parable is the metaphor of generosity disguised or misconstrued as unfairness. At this level, it really *is* all about the landowner's generosity and the new basis of life in community. In other words, it is about the nature of the church. As such, it is not difficult to see how this parable might generate thoughtful reflection and new forms of discipleship in a variety of Christian communities.

We can imagine two possible meanings of the parable, one having to do with Jesus' preference for sinners over the righteous (cf. Matt. 9:13), and the other with the eleventh-hour inclusion of the Gentiles in God's plan of salvation. The first would have characterized the circumstances of Jesus' earthly ministry; the second would have emerged more decisively after it. In his battles with the Pharisees and other parties, it did not go unnoticed that Jesus associated with prostitutes and tax collectors. On the lips of his opponents, this was not a neutral observation but a target for attack. Thus if we follow Jeremias's notion that the story does not hinge on the identity of those hired at 9:00 a.m., noon, and 3:00 p.m. (*Parables of Jesus*, 35) but on the contrast between the first and last hired, it is possible to read the parable as the Lord's answer to those who objected to the radical inclusiveness of his ministry.

Or, again contrasting the earliest and latest workers to be hired, it is possible to interpret those who worked all day in the vineyard as the Jews and the 5:00 p.m. arrivals as Gentiles. Jesus himself prepares for such a reading with his saying against the "heirs of the kingdom" in 8:12 and in his allegory of the Great Feast (Matt.

85

22). The Jew-Gentile reading, then, emerges from the Gospel itself and finds a significant reception in postapostolic and medieval periods. For example, Hilary of Poitiers and Jerome both interpret the worker's grumbling as an expression of Jewish resentment at the inclusion of Gentiles in God's kingdom (Wailes, *Medieval Allegories*, 140).

The church's traditional interpretation was not focused on the dramatic climax of the parable, that is, on the implications of God's grace for the whole community. Instead, it read the parable as an allegory of salvation history with near-exclusive interest in the significance of the various hours at which the laborers are hired. David Steinmetz has provided intriguing snapshots of this exegetical practice from Irenaeus to Luther. Steinmetz observes that in Irenaeus the parable of the Workers in the Vineyard constitutes a commentary on the relationship of Jews and Gentiles in the history of salvation. In Origen, it recounts the various ages in the life of a person at which salvation is possible, with the 5:00 p.m. workers representing late-in-life conversion. Thomas Aquinas, on the other hand, takes the hours to represent the epochs of revelation in world history, from Adam to Christ. In his reading, the workers hired at 5:00 p.m. are the Gentiles whose complaint that no one has hired them means that, unlike the Jews, they have not benefited from the guidance of the prophets. The most poignant and pastoral interpretation is that of the anonymous fourteenth-century poem "Pearl," an elegy on the death of a young girl that compares the lateness of the hour in the parable to a dying child's brief life. God opens the kingdom of heaven to children who have lived in "the vineyard" for but a short time (Steinmetz, "The Superiority of Pre-Critical Exegesis").

What Steinmetz describes in these readings represents the *disciplined* abundance of patristic and medieval exegesis. He demonstrates not only a rich multiplicity of interpretation but also the single fountain from which it emerges:

> It is only against the background of the generosity of God that one can understand the relationship of Jew and Gentile, the problem of late conversion, the meaning of the death of a young child, the question of proportional rewards, even the very definition of grace itself. Every question is qualified by the severe mercy of God, by the strange generosity of the owner of the vineyard who

pays the non-productive latecomer the same wage as his oldest and most productive employees. . . . If you were to ask me which of these interpretations is valid, I should have to respond that they all are. ("Superiority of Pre-Critical Exegesis," 35)

One might add to Steinmetz's judgment that, in the context of Jesus' ministry and Matthew's ecclesial concerns, one can make out certain lines of questioning that will prove more productive than others. If one interprets the parable as an exposition of Jesus' love for sinners in contrast to his religious opponents, we can hear Jesus encouraging the contemporary church to quit resting on the laurels of its own righteousness. If we read the parable as a comment on the inclusion of Gentiles in the kingdom, our attention is drawn to seekers from nontraditional backgrounds, as well as non-Western believers or those from developing nations who have taken a leading role in the global church: Today's "average Anglican" is not a housewife in suburban Connecticut, but a poor woman living in an African village. If the Jews once represented the "veterans" in the vineyard, it is establishment Christians who are now playing that part and who occasionally grumble about it. First-world Christians are already learning that "the last will be first, and the first will be last." Recognition of that truth, repeated throughout the Gospels, stimulates many fruitful questions as well as a certain hermeneutic dexterity. When it comes to the church's mission and the character of our life together, what are the implications of the owner's eccentric generosity?

The parable of the Two Sons in the following chapter captures the same dynamic but in more compact form (Matt. 21:28–32). In this parable, too, the vineyard looms in the background. It is a place of growth and sustenance, but it must be maintained by willing workers. The first son initially refuses his father's command to labor in the vineyard, but later he has a change of heart and obeys; meanwhile the second son says, "I go, sir," but does not set foot in the vineyard. The two sons are not assigned explicit, allegorical meanings, but Jesus' comment on his own parable highlights one of the central contentions of his historical ministry: "Truly I tell you, the tax collectors and the prostitutes [the laborers hired at 5:00 p.m.] are going into the kingdom of God ahead of you" (21:31).

87

Neither of the sons is picture-perfect. Although the first son eventually obeys his father, his initial response is rude and rebellious. The second son is quick to say yes, but he is sneaky and hypocritical, a real disappointment to his father, who has grown gray while dealing with such difficult children. In the shadows and just *out* of the picture, however, stands another son; we may call him the Third Son. He is telling the story with a sad heart. Where the first was rebellious and the second hypocritical, the Third Son is the good child whose initial response is matched by his performance in the vineyard. In him there is not the slightest increment of delay between the Father's command and the son's obedience. "Although he was a Son, he learned obedience through what he suffered" (Heb. 5:8). When we allow the story-*teller* to enter our camera's viewfinder, the meaning of the parable enlarges holistically, much in the way our interpretation of the Treasure in the Field reveals the crucified Christ hidden in a tomb. Not a single detail *in* either of the stories is allegorized, but the veil between the teller and the tale is removed, and everything is clarified. When we read with the eyes of the church, we see three sons instead of two.

The last block of parables in Matthew (chaps. 24–25) shifts our attention to the end of the age. The urgency of these stories reflects their context in the Gospel's overall narrative. Jesus has entered Jerusalem for the last time and is about to be arrested. He has already promised the city of Jerusalem, "I tell you, you will not see me again until you say, 'Blessed is the one who comes in the name of the Lord'" (23:39; cf. 21:9). As in Mark, his prophecy begins with earthly persecutions and religious sacrilege and ends with what appears to be an interpolation of cosmic references to the coming of the Son of Man. Matthew 24:15–44 is the language of apocalypse. In the verses following it, Jesus will assert that it is impossible to know the hour of its fulfillment, but in this section he offers clues. Just as vultures are a sure sign of a corpse nearby, so an assortment of heavenly pyrotechnics will signal the coming of the end. The only question is how to prepare. For that, Jesus returns to parable.

In Matthew's *apocalypse* the Son of Man appears on the clouds with power and glory. In Matthew's *parable* eleven verses later, the Lord comes like a thief in the night. Two traditions are colliding, the former offering the assurance of hope, the latter counseling the need for watchfulness. Each tradition speaks to the spiritual welfare of its recipients. Matthew, therefore, includes both.

The last five parables in Matthew could not be more different from one another in literary form and content, but they all counsel readiness in anticipation of the Lord's return. In the first of these, Jesus says, the situation will be comparable to the times of Noah before the flood, when human beings carried on with life as usual, oblivious to the coming catastrophe. But "if the owner of the house had known in what part of the night the thief was coming, he would have stayed awake and would not have let his house be broken into" (24:43). Even though this brief warning is set in the past tense, it is a similitude, denoting a simple and universal action. It goes without saying that if one knows the exact hour the thief will break in, one will not choose that hour to sleep. The only oddity about this parable occurs not in its bare-bones plot, if it may be called that, but its paradoxical imagery: the Son of Man as thief! When addressing the faithful, the New Testament deems the second coming to be an event of redemption, but its agent, who might well have worn the mantle of a conquering hero or a victorious athlete, is represented by the despised figure of a robber, about whom the book of Job says, "The murderer rises at dusk, . . . and in the night is like a thief" (Job 24:14). The point of comparison has nothing to do with the immorality of stealing but with the "overtones" that attend the act of breaking and entering. A contemporary preacher manages to honor these overtones in her sermon "God's Beloved Thief," in which she asserts a double point of comparison. The coming of the Thief is characterized by the unexpected nature of his arrival *and* the total access he has to the stuff of our lives (Taylor, "God's Beloved Thief," 3–9).

Matthew follows with a longer parable in 24:45–51. The nature of Jesus' question, "Who then is the faithful and wise slave?" immediately challenges the hearer to identify with the smart, reliable slave as opposed to the wicked, misbehaving slave. The question is not, "Are you a slave?" but "What kind of slave will you be?" Like "servant" in the Old Testament and the Gospels, "slave" probably represents the spiritual leaders of the fledgling Jesus community. The good slave is both reliable and, like the followers of Jesus, lives at complete disposal to the will of the owner (see the continuing discussion of "parabolic slaves" in chap. 5 below). The wicked slave makes two sorts of mistakes: the first is his bad behavior, drunkenness, and cruelty; the second, more comprehensive mistake is to think his master will not come. When the master unexpectedly shows up, the bad slave will be very sorry indeed.

89

Matthew has arranged these final five parables in an ascending order of literary complexity. So far, he has progressed from a similitude to a parable and now, in chapter 25, from a brief allegory, to a much longer allegory, and finally to a sermon. In the parable of the Wise and Foolish Bridesmaids (25:1–13), it is no longer a master but the more theologically explicit "bridegroom," whom we have already met in Matthew 9:15 and in the parable of the Great Feast in chapter 22. Like the master in other parables, the bridegroom is inexplicably delayed and, like a thief, he arrives in the middle of the night to shouted welcomes. The foolish five have brought no oil; the wise five have kept their oil with them; but in what appears to be an empirical observation on the part of the narrator, "all of them became drowsy and slept" (25:5). The delay of the Parousia is such that all will be lulled to distraction; our preoccupations with other affairs, however, must be underlaid by a basic conviction that will enable believers to respond faithfully when the hour comes. This is a mark of the kingdom not revealed in the early phases of Jesus' ministry: readiness.

The black church in America has a saying, "There is such a thing as 'Too Late.'" The five foolish bridesmaids are reminiscent of the global-warming doubters in the book of Genesis who didn't make it into Noah's ark. When the door closed on them, they were sorry, but it was too late. Earlier in Matthew's Gospel, Jesus says the complacent children of the kingdom will not make it to the heavenly table with Abraham, Isaac, and Jacob. Their replacements will come from east and west and the realms beyond Israel (8:11–12). When the foolish bridesmaids miss their meeting with the groom, they are also missing out on Abraham, Isaac, Jacob, and the eschatological banquet to come.

The parable of the Talents (25:14–30) draws on the same themes, but the allegory is thematically developed and embellished by characterization and dialogue. The story has a fairy-tale quality, especially in its tripartite division of talents, but the dialogue in the second half of the parable helps offset its formulaic structure. In this parable, the Jesus figure is a man going on a journey (back to the Father?), who first summons his slaves and entrusts "his property" to three of them in the form of five, two, and one talents respectively. There is nothing arbitrary or random in this arrangement, for the shares of responsibility have been carefully assessed and apportioned "to each according to his ability." The story is best imagined as oral performance. The first two slaves invest successfully; they and the master make what are essentially the same two speeches. Indeed, the first two slaves stand for one faithful response. The audience, sensing that these two are not where the action is, waits apprehensively for the other shoe to drop. It does so in the form of new and extended dialogue, a profound psychological profile of the slave who buried his talent in the ground, and an explosion of judgment on the part of the master.

This is not a happy story. It is a cautionary tale addressed to those entrusted with the Lord's work, but who lack the courage to embrace its inherent value for the purposes of growth in the kingdom of heaven. We don't really know the bridesmaids, and we are not given even the smallest window into their personalities. But in the third slave we meet someone we know. He is not in control of his own life or body, and he knows he can be hurt by a bad decision. After all, he is a slave. His cautious conservatism is presented in a way that is familiar to us, his nonslave successors. "Master," the third slave whines, "I knew that you were a harsh man, reaping where you did not sow, and gathering where you did not scatter seed; so I was afraid, and I went and hid your talent in the ground." "Here," he says, handing his master a damp and muddy piece of silver, "you have what is yours." From that speech we can extrapolate a powerful conflict in the third slave between trust in the goodness of the gift and fear of the wrath of the giver. These two options represent two motivations of a very different sort. One is the embrace of risk, the other is a desire for security, and both are alive and well in the church.

Churches will occasionally use this parable as a motivational tool for raising money. In these cases the emphasis usually falls on the resources of individual members (not usually identified as "slaves"!) who are categorized by talent or financial endowment as five-talent, two-talent, or one-talent persons. They are then exhorted to produce results not in accordance with the grace of God, but in proportion to their talents. What the church sometimes forgets is that the story is a parable, not an example story. The "talents" do not denote our peculiar abilities or resources but refer to dispensations of grace that belong to God and come only from God. What is being invested is not *my* money, *my* valuable time, or *my* extraordinary expertise, but the generously bestowed blessings of God. It is only on that basis that Jesus can warn of a "talent" being taken from one

91

and given to others, much in the way Paul suggests that the many gifts made to Israel have been transferred to the Gentiles (Rom. 11). All the gifts of God work that way. One does not hoard, hide, or bury the promises, the sacraments, ministry, joy, hope, justice, witness, suffering, salvation, or reconciliation. What the third slave did is, strictly speaking, impossible, for when the gifts are buried, they cease to exist. The parable suggests a reckoning larger than an assessment of an individual's abilities or annual pledge. The true reckoning awaits the entire community, whose faithfulness in ministry is judged every day, and one day will be judged definitively. After that it will be "too late."

The literary escalation of these five parables in Matthew 24–25 reaches its climax in the Judgment of the Nations (25:31–46). I have called it a sermon because it preaches the very reckoning we have been talking about: the last, authoritative, universal clarification of everything Jesus has been pointing to in the previous four parables. It lacks the character of a true parable because from the very beginning it is both prophecy and the explication of prophecy in the same literary unit. In it Jesus unveils the kingdom that has always been there from the beginning. Despite so much of the church's rhetoric, we have not been "building the kingdom" after all, for the reign of God is now being uncovered (which is the root meaning of "revelation") in the most unlikely of scenarios. The bright lights and heavenly clouds have dissipated, and what is left is a tender recognition scene. As it turns out, many of our metaphors for the kingdom have been off the mark. God's reign is not really a force or an energy, not something that bursts like a bombshell or succeeds like a business. The kingdom was born in love "from the foundation of the world" and prepared for those who "are blessed," as a home or a room is prepared for the beloved child (25:34). Jesus says to his followers, It is "for you," which in terms of Reformation theology renders the kingdom of God as an expression of the gospel. These words, "for you," assure believers that the dawning of the kingdom brings not terror but joy and a settled peace.

Even in this most public of judgment scenes, the truth of the kingdom is oddly hidden. For the righteous have had no idea of the criteria by which they would be judged. Their (our) judgment comes in an intersection with the suffering of others. If we want to know what the five, two, and single talents stand for in the parable of the Talents, we have our answer in the simple acts of ministry

92

outlined in this sermon. The clueless righteous are dumbfounded, first, to discover that they are being judged by their acts of mercy toward the less fortunate brothers and sisters of the Lord. Second, they are astonished as they watch the outer shell of these same people of God dissolving before their eyes, only to reveal the presence of Jesus within them. The lonely old man, the cancer-stricken woman, the kid in the county prison—Jesus. The righteous ask, "Lord, when was it that we saw you hungry and gave you food . . . ?" It says something good about them, I think, that they can't calculate the theological significance of their acts of mercy. Jesus says in effect, "You don't remember, but I remember." No theologian better captures the fusion of persons than Julian of Norwich, who in her "Parable of the Lord and Servant" (in *Revelations of Divine Love*, chap. 51) makes no distinction between Christ and suffering humanity. We shall consider her "reading" of the parables in the concluding chapter (below).

Matthew 25 is the final demonstration. In this unveiling, love for the Lord and works of mercy meet and kiss one another. The many Christians who are fascinated by times and seasons, dates and dispensations, who find the European Union and Cobra helicopters in the book of Revelation—these fortune-tellers are given a simple answer to their complex speculations. Here also the more sophisticated among us, who keep the Lord at arm's length by means of theological abstractions such as "eschatology" or "apocalyptic," are invited to open their eyes to this uncovering, for in the hungry, poor, alien, sick, and imprisoned brother or sister we all stand before Jesus in the ultimate reckoning. History ends in the glory of this vision.

Matthew's narrative, on the other hand, turns to a crucifixion.

The Gospel of Luke

Earlier, I characterized Luke's parables as missional and literary. They are missional in the broadest sense of the word, depicting the thrust and contours of life in the kingdom of God. His parables are worldly, in the sense that they accurately reflect the ambiguities of the Christian life, to which Luke usually offers no pat resolution. He has virtually no allegories, which means he is less interested than Matthew in nailing down theological positions and more concerned that his readers identify with and experience the challenges of life in the kingdom of God. Luke favors what critics call the "example story," such as the parable of Lazarus and the Rich Man or the Good Samaritan; yet even in the most straightforward example story, a twist of uncertainty remains. On the whole, his longer stories contain a greater complexity of plot, psychological depth of conflict, and more descriptive detail than we are accustomed to in the Gospel of Matthew. Finally, his literary realism stands out against the formulaic language and cartoonish details of Matthew's allegories. Luke's characters are recognizable to our culture, and their dilemmas confirm the modern reader's experience. Their dreams, foibles, and complaints are familiar to us. Unlike Matthew, Luke manages to avoid clumsy or wooden introductions to the parables and integrates them more organically into the larger narrative of Jesus' ministry. Of course, some critics contend that this is a weakness on Luke's part, since his framing of the parables occasionally betrays his own misunderstanding of the material he has received.

A good example of his organic style occurs at 14:7, where Luke introduces a thematic section on banqueting: "When he noticed how the guests chose the places of honor, he told them a parable." Jesus observes human behavior at a fancy dinner, and it reminds him of a story—three stories, actually. The first two are example stories that reflect the values of the kingdom of God. The first, in 14:8–11, contains commonsense advice on seating arrangements at a dinner. If you're not sure, it's best to take the lowest place at the banquet, because a public upgrade is always better than a public humiliation. The second example story, in 14:12–14, is of a more radical nature, for it flies in the face of common sense and ordinary practice. He says, "When you give a luncheon or a dinner, do not invite your friends or your brothers or your relatives or rich neighbors [which nearly exhausts most people's guest lists], in case they may invite you in return [which is everyone's social strategy]. . . . But when you give a banquet, invite the poor, the crippled, the lame, and the blind [which never happens, but for which the communion table provides a practice run]." These are example stories and not "true" parables, but such a judgment does not dull their theological value. They are not about hospitality or good manners or any other virtue separable from the radical new way of life in the kingdom of God. We do not need to allegorize these humble stories

94

in order to make them more doctrinally explicit; we need only to live them.

Chapter 14 includes a third and final banquet story (vv. 15–24), which we have already considered in a previous chapter. Luke seamlessly integrates the final parable into his banquet framework by having one of the guests who, upon hearing the first two stories, provides the theological setup for the third story: "Blessed is anyone who will eat bread in the kingdom of God!" Jesus responds with the parable of the Great Feast. It is a true parable in that the complexities of its action offer a figurative enactment of three phases in the story of salvation: God's desire to gather all to the kingdom, humankind's rejection of that offer, and God's persistent love for those who, in the mysterious ordering of things, were not included in the original invitation. In Matthew's version the refusals "explain" God's rejection of an entire people and evoke an over-the-top reaction on the part of the king, but in Luke there is no violence, and the emphasis remains on the host's gracious invitation. In Matthew we have no mention of the poor, the crippled, the blind, and the lame, as in Luke 14:21, and nothing of the host's desire for a full house. The parable of the Great Feast sets the scene for chapter 15 and the greater feast of love.

Of the parables we have not already discussed, the most important are found in "the gospel within the Gospel," so named because chapter 15 contains the purest and most compelling narrative portrayals of God's love for sinners found in the New Testament. They are stories of a lost sheep, a lost coin, and a lost boy.

As is his custom, Luke neatly frames the similitude of the Lost Sheep by observing that the tax collectors and sinners have gathered around Jesus, while the grumbling scribes and Pharisees form an outer ring of the audience. Jesus introduces his subject with a direct question, "Which one of you, having a hundred sheep . . . ?" The parable is meant to be overheard by those in the outer ring, and its lesson is for them to learn. There is no need to allegorize the sheep or the shepherd or to speculate on what might happen to the ninety-nine if left alone or to moralize on the virtues of persistence.

We can identify three features of this brief story: The narrative action remains centered on the listener/reader. There is no Good Shepherd—there is no shepherd at all—but only "one of you." Jesus skillfully includes his hearers in a story about someone else's search-and-rescue mission, with the result that it becomes

95

the hearers' story. Instead of preaching a sermon about love, he exhibits it by means of two narrative gestures. The first is an action that by any modern standard of evangelization fails the test of cost-effectiveness. Beginning with the prophets and continuing in the Gospels, ministry is portrayed as a sending forth. In Isaiah 6:8 the Lord asks, "Whom shall I send, and who will go for us?" In the New Testament, the pattern continues as God sends John the Baptizer, and then Jesus, and Jesus sends his followers. In the Sending of the Seventy in Luke 10, the mission may be schematized as follows:

sending → witnessing → returning → rejoicing

The sequence is not a Lukan invention but a Lukan discovery of an older and more deeply ingrained pattern of mission. In Luke 15 the evangelist has altered it to read:

searching → finding → returning → rejoicing

The ministry of seeking, as opposed to the "Let them find us on our website" theory of mission, is notoriously inefficient. Demographically based mission operations and virtual evangelism will fill up the building, but will such methods turn up the lost soul?

The second gesture of love in this little story is even more telling: in an act of undeclared affection, the man lays the sheep across his shoulders. He doesn't drive it with a stick, but he *carries* it home. With this gesture and his rejoicing, the party begins while the man and his sheep are still in the wilderness. The rejoicing will continue at home with friends and neighbors and, Jesus adds, in heaven.

Since we are reading with Luke, we might notice in passing that we are no longer reading with Matthew, who includes the same parable but uses it for a different purpose. It appears as a part of Matthew's discussion of forgiveness and church discipline in chapter 18, where it does not serve the purpose of outreach but reclamation. Unlike the version found in Matthew 18:10–14, where Jesus' concern is for the "little ones" and those who have gone "astray" (Greek *planōmenon*), in Luke 15 the story is performed in the presence of hardened outsiders, "sinners," who qualify as "lost" (Greek *apolōlos*). In Matthew, one senses that the sheep have strayed from "the church" (cf. v. 15); in Luke, the ninety-nine are no less beloved to the one searching for them, but they are lost in a more "distant country" (cf. v.

96

13). Although in each Gospel the search is marked by the same intensive care, Matthew's is pastoral in character and Luke's is missionary. In Matthew the rejoicing is muted at best; in Luke, approximately 60 percent of the narrative is devoted to celebration and joy.

The parable of the Lost Coin is an example of Luke's practice of alternating between male and female protagonists (cf. 7:1–17). However, just as we do not have the Good Shepherd in the previous story, we do not have the Good Housewife in this one. In keeping with his preference for anonymous, universal characters, Luke does not idealize her personal qualities but introduces her only as "what woman" (15:8). In several respects the parables of the Lost Sheep and the Lost Coin are mirror images of one another. Both are similitudes; both depict a persistent search for something of relatively minor value that has been lost, and both end in a neighborhood party. Where each parable exceeds the ordinary is in the eruption of joy at the discovery of something as insignificant as one sheep in a hundred or one drachma in ten—or one lost soul who repents.

At the divinity school where I teach, a life-sized bronze sculpture of three figures stands in the center of the courtyard. An older man bends and broods over two figures before him. One is on his knees, his head buried at his father's waist; the other is tensed and stands apart as if to distance himself from the scene. His arms are folded across his chest, and his face and body are taut. With one arm around the kneeling boy and the other on the standing figure's shoulder, the father appears to hold the tableaux together. The sculpture is visible from several classrooms, the refectory, and faculty offices. It is as central to the meaning of our life together as the parable of the Prodigal Son is to the Gospel of Luke.

In comparison with the simplicity of the two previous similitudes, the parable of the Prodigal Son, or the Lost Boy, reads like a short story, for it contains a developed plot with not one but two major conflicts, several scene changes, three important characters, characterization, dialogue, interior monologue, and a speech. Its plot may appear to be the same as the two preceding similitudes, but it is not, because the features I have enumerated transform structure into story and produce a very different aesthetic experience for the reader. In each of the similitudes, for example, Jesus mentions repentance. Yet neither a sheep nor a coin can repent. But a boy can repent, and this parable allows the reader to watch and feel the birth of repentance in the consciousness of one lost soul.

97

The first scene introduces the formulaic threesome found in many European fairy tales: a father and two sons. For all practical purposes, they are the only characters in the story. The younger son asks for his share of the inheritance in advance, which is tantamount to leveling his father with a death wish. The second scene finds the son in a distant country, where he has squandered his inheritance by living "dissolutely," a Greek word whose root meaning is "unsavingly," or "in a way beyond saving." His behavior, beginning with his disrespect for his father, has effectively put him in a situation beyond redemption. The third scene is a pigsty, in which he gladly would have eaten the pods intended for the pigs. In that condition he comes to himself, realizing that even his father's hired hands back home are eating better than he is. This is a rare scene of mimetic power in the New Testament, for the speaker/writer is providing an interior snapshot of the process by which a mind changes and a life is redirected. No other story in the Gospels takes its reader into the heart of a character as does the parable of the Prodigal Son.

The impetus for the young man's turn of mind has as much to do with his empty stomach as his newly warmed heart. In the literature of alcoholism and drug abuse, such scenes and soliloquies are common. One day the alcoholic looks in the mirror and is granted a moment of self-recognition so devastatingly accurate and so rife with self-loathing as to be jolted into action. The Prodigal begins rehearsing a speech he will never give in its entirety. It is as if the boy "comes to himself" (cf. 15:17) and immediately realizes he needs a better speech with which to satisfy his father. Although he is making the turn toward home, he still does not fully comprehend the unconditional love of the father, who requires no speeches and apparently doesn't care *why* the boy is coming home as long as he comes home.

The next scene unfolds at the end of the long road leading to his house. There is nothing like the pathos of this scene in any of Gospels, with the exception of the post-resurrection scene between Jesus and Mary Magdalene in the Fourth Gospel. The father spies him at a distance and, breaking Near Eastern protocol, runs to him, embraces him, and kisses him. The son begins the speech he has rehearsed, but the father's forgiveness cuts it short with orders to his slaves to prepare a great celebration. The celebration does not reinstate the son to his father's love, for "this son of mine," as he calls him, was *never* anything but a son to him. As in the previous two parables, the story ends with communal rejoicing.

98

After three consecutive parables of searching, forgiveness, restoration, and joy, the reader of Luke's Gospel can have no doubt about God's abiding love for the lost. And since all three are framed by Jesus' radical ministry to tax collectors and sinners, Jesus, too, is deeply implicated in the same love. As the Father's emissary, he is enacting the same sequence of search, forgive, and celebrate, but at a cost that has not yet been revealed. It seems a perfect place to end the story.

But the man has *two* sons.

It is a mark of Luke's narrative skill that, in respect to the other son, he induces a momentary amnesia in the reader, with the result that the elder son's appearance comes as something of a shock. The older boy approaches the house, and once again the father comes out to meet his son. The father has never been indifferent to him; nor is his love for the older son any less intense than what he has lavished on his younger brother. Even their financial arrangement is identical, for when the younger boy demanded his inheritance, the father divided his property between *them* (15:12). The elder brother has not been working as a hired hand or a "slave," as he bitterly complains. Thanks to his little brother's stupidity and his father's generosity, he is a stakeholder in the farm.

His father pleads with him to come in, but to no avail. He identifies the younger boy only as "this brother of yours," but the older son rhetorically blocks the thought by referring to him as "this son of yours." In a burst of sibling overkill, he fleshes out the meaning of "dissolute living" by accusing his brother of consorting with prostitutes. He makes his speech while standing at the threshold of "home," his own true home, but as Clarence Jordan observes in a sermon, because the older son cannot reconcile with his brother, he has no choice but to turn his back on his father. Which is to walk away from the light, the music, and the joy of his father's house.

The story of the elder son is a metaphor for every good person who has done his or her duty and kept the faith without the expectation of reward, only to be badly stung when those who have done far less are made the object of joy. This is also the dynamic and dilemma of the Workers in the Vineyard (Matt. 20). Like the owner of the vineyard, the father does not love one son above the other, and he does not reward one above the other. For those who toiled in the vineyard all day, the equality of reward was hard to take. For the elder son, it is the father's *joy* that cuts and galls.

99

The elder son has many faces. He is the faithful Jew who in Luke's Gospel will look on in dismay as Jesus showers affection on the Gentiles, whose disappointment cannot be mollified by the father's assurance: "Son, you are always with me, and all that is mine is yours." As Paul puts it, "To them [the Jews] belong the adoption, the glory, the covenants, the giving of the law, the worship, and the promises" (Rom. 9:4). The elder son is the Pharisee and scribe, not only miffed but outraged and threatened by what they see being done to their religion. The elder son is the Good Christian from the Bible belt, or the liberal Episcopalian, Presbyterian, or Lutheran, who is baffled and not a little irritated by the rising authority of churches in the Global South. The elder son shakes his head at his own congregation's embrace of people he has always disapproved of. The elder son is the church-going deacon who believes that because he has never been to a literal far country, he has never been lost. The elder son is any believer whose prosaic goodness has never been turned to poetry in a public celebration. The elder son is the best of us at our very worst.

We can become so involved in the drama of the parable that we lose sight of the part it plays in Luke's portrait of the kingdom of God. The parable of the elder son is not merely a codicil to a more satisfying story. Theologically, it reminds us that being "found" in the kingdom means more than a joyous celebration of a new relationship with the Father. The story is only completed when all those who have been found are reconciled to one another. But the elder son doesn't have it in him to put his arms around his brother and to kiss him. The ecstasy of being found is "squandered," to use a good Lukan word (15:13), by the elder brother's failure to love. For lack of reconciliation, the story remains open-ended, unfinished, and sad. We can hear the music, but it is distant and someone is missing.

The next parable in the Gospel of Luke appears to offer a complete change of pace. The lovable characters and pathos of self-discovery in the parable of the Prodigal Son have evaporated in the heat of a financial crisis. It is the parable of the Dishonest Steward, whose story comes to us courtesy of the business school rather than the divinity school or chapel. It is often referred to as "the hardest parable."

100   It is hard because the reader cannot decide whether to assign a positive or a negative value to the steward's behavior. Modern translations prefer to think of him as "Shrewd" instead of the traditional

and more judgmental "Dishonest." "Shrewd" we can admire, "Dishonest" we cannot. The parable does reveal a shrewdness of behavior that passes for dexterity in the marketplace, and the Greek *phronimōs* in verse 8 carries classical overtones of practical wisdom. But by the end of the story the original judgment stands, and Jesus himself nails the essence of the man: he is *adikias* (unjust, unrighteous; v. 8).

The puzzle of the parable turns on the master's approval of a person who is *adikias*. No one, including the evangelist, understands exactly what Jesus was getting at with this story, but I believe that if we read the core of the parable in 16:1–8 within the framework of Luke's Gospel, we will make a good start.

Structurally, the original parable of the Dishonest Steward has the same plot as the Prodigal Son. The two of them share the following structural elements: (1) an unlikable and morally ambiguous protagonist; (2) a crisis provoked by the protagonist's questionable actions; (3) a descent into chaos; (4) the protagonist's chastened reflection on his true state of affairs, as revealed by means of interior monologue; (5) a decisive turn of behavior; (6) a yearning to be welcomed "home"; and finally, (7) the father-figure's reward and approval. No need to diagram it: they are the same story.

Moreover, Luke positions the parable immediately after (or as a mirror image of) the parable of the Prodigal Son. In the first verse he repeats the same verb used to describe the Prodigal's behavior in the far country: "squander" (Greek *dieskorpisen*, 15:13; *diaskorpizōn*, 16:1; cf. Donahue, *Gospel in Parable*, 167). From a structural point of view, they may be the same story, but the latter is more difficult to interpret for several reasons. First and foremost, the second parable goes out of its way to cast the protagonist in a dubious moral light. Apparently the steward has already accumulated a bad work history, and now it has caught up with him. Like the Prodigal, who compares his position in the pigsty with that of his father's hired hands, the steward makes a realistic self-assessment—one that continues to resonate with middle-management types, academics, and the clergy: "I am not strong enough to dig, and I am ashamed to beg" (16:3). The parable allows us to assume that he has been inflating prices in order to skim a sweet commission for himself. The only solution open to him is to deflate the debts by the amount of his personal margin of profit and perhaps a bit more. This he does, taking care to have his customers put it in their own handwriting in the event

101

of an audit. Everyone is happy: the clients like the lower prices, the master is delighted with full payment, and the steward has managed (barely) to dodge the outer darkness. Yet even by the end of the story, the steward has not been promoted to a grade above *adikias*. "The master commended the dishonest steward for his shrewdness" (16:8 RSV). This is not what the pious reader expects, since "the master" in many of these stories is a God figure.

Even more confusing, the Master who is telling this tawdry little tale—*not* the character of the rich man in the narrative, but Jesus—appears to approve of the manager's behavior. (Verse 8, master = *ho kyrios*, retains the ambiguity, though most interpreters believe that *kyrios* here refers to the character *in* the story and not its Teller; the NRSV advocates this view by mistranslating the sentence to read, "And *his* master commended the dishonest manager" [emphasis added]). The Jesus who tells this murky story is the same Jesus who in another place in Luke's Gospel says unambiguously, "If you lend to those from whom you hope to receive, what credit is that to you? Even sinners lend to sinners, to receive as much again" (Luke 6:34). The Lord who appears to countenance the steward's behavior is himself the very antithesis of a shrewd wheeler-dealer. At his every opportunity to save himself, he chooses not to do so. Thus our conundrum: the one who approves of the steward's shrewdness will die on a cross as the personification of Anti-Shrewd. Moreover, it's not as if the steward has rescued the master's money for the kingdom of God, the church, or some other worthy cause. The question of ends and means doesn't enter into the equation because he's done it only to save his own hide.

After all this, Jesus seems to say, "Okay, on some days, this is what the kingdom can be like. Please remember, this is a *parable*, not an allegory or an example story. Do not read it as a manual on business ethics or church development!"

One of the problems in interpreting the parable has to do with the moral and theological lens through which we view it. The generations of Christians who have separated faith from worldly involvement are offended by the steward's behavior. Others, like us, who secretly wish we were half so dexterous and cannot but admire the rogue who always lands on his feet, can only agree with the master's commendation. Those who define the church by its contrast with the world will not like the core of this parable. Those who view the church as a "player" in this world, for whom "entrepreneurial

Christianity" is not a contradiction in terms, will admire the steward's ability to get the job done.

The steward is a liminal figure, neither a child of the night or of the day, but of the twilight, where there is just enough light to get by. We want to have this parable both ways, and we manage it by separating the content of the steward's dubious actions from the resourcefulness with which he carries them out. When our moral strategy is applied to other figures, such as sports cheaters, murderers, or crooks like Bernard Madoff, the silliness of this approach is quickly unmasked. Both Luther and Wesley follow this line of interpretation: Luther, in a sermon titled "The Holy Swindler" (cited in Sittler, "Unjust Steward," 227); and Wesley, who argues that the master commended the steward because "he used timely precaution." Wesley goes on to articulate a "rule" enunciated by Jesus in his explanation of the parable: "Gain *all* you can, by common sense, by using in your business all the understanding which God has given you" ("Use of Money," in *Works*, 2:273).

More recently, Christian "realists," such as Reinhold Niebuhr, have reflected on the role of morality in politics and social policy. In *The Children of Light and the Children of Darkness* (a title suggested by Luke 16:8), Niebuhr criticizes the children of darkness for their cynical use of power, but also the "foolish" children of light for their sentimentality in worldly matters. Niebuhr's position implicitly baptizes the steward's behavior as an example of the ways in which self-interest coexists with noble behavior and may bring about a positive outcome (9–13). The steward never abjectly repents in the truest sense of the word, but then, even in the Prodigal's rehearsed speech we have discerned a hint of insincerity. No one is perfect, especially Christians who have not recused themselves from political or economic engagement with the world. On this side of paradise, the realists argue, the kingdom will continue to rely on flawed characters and morally compromised methods in order to make its witness in the world.

On the other side are the "absolutists," for whom the figure of the amoral steward is reprehensible. According to their interpretation, Jesus is not admiring the children of this age but contrasting them with the children of light. They see an unstated principle in Luke 16:1–8: "If the children of this age are capable of shrewd and profitable actions, *how much more* will the children of light be blessed in the world to come." While the realists divide the parable

103

morally, the absolutists divide it structurally by largely ignoring the parable proper and focusing on the sermonic chiding that follows it.

If we view the parable through the lens of its structural components enumerated above, it yields a less reproachful conclusion. Without the editorial interpretation in verses 9–13, Luke 16:1–8 tells the story of a man whose sins bring him to a terrible crisis, who makes a few desperate course corrections (as does the Prodigal in the previous story), and who finally receives the commendation of his superior. Just as God welcomes tax collectors, prostitutes, and other lost souls into the kingdom, so God also opens the doors of heaven to middle-management types, tax cheats, and other reprobates. If we were to examine the inner lives and actual behavior of prostitutes, tax collectors, and other friends of Jesus, as Luke permits us to do with the Dishonest Steward, we might not be thrilled to sit down at table with them in the kingdom of God. However, only the prodigals and crooks appear to have responded to Jesus' message with repentance. To the professional religionists, Jesus says, "You did not recognize the time of your visitation" (Luke 19:44).

We think we know what the kingdom of God looks like. It looks like the Baptist Church, the Episcopal hierarchy, the Methodist system, Presbyterian polity, Lutheran liturgy, Catholic tradition, or religious sentiment. But what if the kingdom is the crying need for a homeless shelter, food pantry, hospitality center, or some other vehicle of God's urgent demand upon us? Who among us has not admired leaders of the "faith community" who twist arms, scratch backs, call in favors, and use their God-given connections for a good cause? They pull it off with a lack of piety that would have made the (M)aster proud.

If we overlook a few unsavory points on the steward's record, and grade him only on a pass-fail basis, he barely earns a pass. But in the kingdom of God, *barely* is more than enough to set off a huge celebration.

Yet there is more to the parable, and that is its second crux of interpretation. In 16:9–13, Luke presents Jesus' gloss on his own story, in which he appears to trade commendation of the steward for condemnation. Virtually all interpreters consider these verses to be Lukan additions, since they have little to do with the complexities of the parable itself, verse 9 being a possible exception: "Make friends for yourselves by means of dishonest wealth so that when it [the money] is gone, they [your new friends] may welcome

104

you into the eternal homes." Those who do the work of the kingdom presumably hope to be received into the eternal habitations, along with those whom they have served. In the parable, verse 9 incorporates that truth but with an ironic touch. The steward does secure a future for himself by making friends, but only because of his dishonest dealings on their behalf. The evangelist's moral sends a mixed message at best: it offers the reader no way out of the paradox and therefore no way forward.

The saying about dishonesty in verse 10 appears to reference the steward's fiddling with the books: whoever is dishonest in the little things cannot be trusted in greater matters, which is true enough but inapplicable to the story.

Verses 11 and 12 suggest that financial dishonesty is a disqualifying factor when it comes to greater, spiritual responsibilities.

The saying in verse 13 about the impossibility of serving God and mammon did not originally belong to the parable. "No slave can serve two masters; for a slave will either hate the one and love the other, or be devoted to the one and despise the other. You cannot serve God and wealth." It is a logion that in the Gospel of Matthew appears in an entirely different context (cf. Matt. 6:24). If the reader does not grasp the figurative nature of the comparison, the image of slaves and masters makes no sense. For slaves, the notion of a freely made choice of masters does not exist, and wealth— mammon—is not an option for them. Thus the saying is not about personal choices made by upwardly mobile individuals like us. Marcus Borg reads it as an indictment of the class system in Palestine; I read it more specifically as an unconscious mitigation of the steward's actions, who in the bounded economic world of the parable is only doing what he has to do (see chap. 5 below; Borg, *Jesus in Scholarship*, 104).

Finally, in verse 14, which is not usually included in the parable's interpretation, Luke goes to great lengths to make it clear that this is a story about money: "The Pharisees, who were lovers of money, heard all this, and they ridiculed him." Why they ridicule him for such a story is unclear. If they really are lovers of money, they should love the story of the resourceful steward.

What are we to make of Luke's confusing array of sermons in verses 9–13? Do these warnings reflect a series of financial scandals in the early church? We do not know, but we should notice that Luke returns to the subject several times in the book of Acts. In

105

sum, we have five bonus verses with four heavy-handed sermonic judgments, none of which speaks directly to the moral ambiguity of the parable itself. The added commentary is sharply critical of the steward's methods and highly moralistic in character. None of them, however, acknowledges the longer curve in the story of the steward's adventure and the structure of salvation hidden in it.

If we continue to read the parable of the Dishonest Steward as a companion piece to the Prodigal Son, what does Luke's gloss mean? It means that good people have a harder time comprehending grace than those who are in desperate need of it. The Elder Brother is the Good Man who doesn't have a theory of grace and therefore can only resent God's undeserved mercy shown to others. But in the parable of the Dishonest Steward, no Elder Brother appears to object to the steward's methods or the master's leniency. *There is only Luke.* His editorial response parallels that of the Elder Brother in the parable of the Prodigal Son. The evangelist unwittingly casts himself in the role of the disapproving, resentful religionist who cannot tolerate moral ambiguity among the faithful and who therefore cannot bring himself to join in the master's celebratory comments. Matthew would have been proud of Luke's effort to protect the community from crooks, and especially so tainted a character as the Dishonest Steward.

Before we leave this parable, we must ask how the Evangelist of Grace managed to miss the grace dispensed to the shady operator, the steward, in this parable. And by drawing attention to Luke's disapproving comments, have I subtly shifted from reading "with Luke" to reading "against Luke"? I believe I am still reading with the evangelist, but I have noticed that he is one of us and that we have more in common with him than we wish to acknowledge. For even gospel-centered, progressive evangelicals (like us) occasionally find themselves reading with the Elder Brother rather than the Forgiving Father. In assuming that certain types of sins and classes of sinners are beyond the pale of redemption, we master the libretto of the gospel but miss its music.

The editorial comments on dishonesty and the Pharisees' love of money provide a somewhat tenuous segue to one of Luke's most celebrated parables, the parable of Lazarus and the Rich Man. Like the parable of the Prodigal Son, this parable features multiple settings and broadly sketched characters. Tales of the rich and the poor in the afterlife are found in many traditions: an Egyptian story

106

similar to this one predated Jesus' parable (Hultgren, *Parables of Jesus*, 111). Unlike the story of the Prodigal, the two characters represent social types and have little psychological depth to them. "There was a rich man." Helmut Thielicke observes, "These words themselves indicate that there is something wrong in the life of this man," for it is "a terrible thing if the only and the ultimate statement that can be made about a person is that he was 'rich'" (*Waiting Father*, 42). The reason for the typecasting has to do with the fable-like genre of the parable, which includes rueful observations about life and death that are dispatched from the realm of the afterlife. Nine of the story's twelve verses take place either in heaven or hell.

Although many of the church's greatest preachers have used this parable to promote almsgiving, Jesus does not in so many words command generosity to the poor. The rich man does not abuse Lazarus; he is simply *there* in his own world, hermetically sealed off from the suffering of the poor. Nor is Lazarus painted in particularly virtuous colors; he too is simply *there*, lying by the gate in a derelict world that is still recognizable to us. Among the tribes in northern Natal in South Africa, the most common greeting is *sawu bona*, literally, "I see you," to which the other replies, "I am here" (recounted in Sims, *Servanthood*, 6). As the rich man looks out his double-paned window at the impressive entrance to his mansion, his mantra is "*I don't see you.*" And the poor man on the sidewalk responds to no one in particular, "*I am not seen.*" While Lazarus's poverty suggests nothing about his character, he does gain favor in the eyes of God by means of his poverty. Not as a virtue but as a condition that violates something in God or in God's creation.

In some Old Testament passages the poor are grammatically incorporated into God's identity: Who is your God? It is the God "*who* . . . raises the poor from the dust, and lifts the needy from the ash heap" (Ps. 113:7). God does not love the poor because they are good but because they are low. And they respond to God not because they are good but because they have no other source of help. In the background of this story stands the prophets' massive testimony to God's care for the poor. Next to the sin of idolatry, responsibility for the poor is the chief topic of prophetic discourse. Whether this story constitutes God's "preferential option for the poor" we may leave to the rich man in hell to decide. Luke has already made up his mind in the Magnificat:

107

> He has brought down the powerful from their thrones,
>   and lifted up the lowly;
> he has filled the hungry with good things,
>   and sent the rich away empty.
>
> (1:52–53)

Despite the narrative's powerful resonances to the prophetic tradition, the parable of Lazarus and the Rich Man is not an example story meant to encourage better behavior in the kingdom of God. Without a doubt, it witnesses to the abundance of poverty in our own backyard among people we no longer notice. But in the ultimate fate of the rich man, known to tradition as Dives (Latin for "rich"), it also teaches the poverty of abundance, for wealth establishes its own insulation from the poor and therefore contains the seeds of its own undoing. Dives cannot buy his way out of hell. The parable speaks to well-off individuals and churches, which, though not exotically rich by Western standards, are insulated from the suffering of others by the many accoutrements of abundance. It is addressed to religious communities that have inherited the biblical language of poverty and lavishly appointed churches in which to talk about it.

But the story is more than a cautionary tale. The parable of Lazarus and the Rich Man is a true parable of reversal in which the very nature of the kingdom is revealed. As Thielicke says in his sermon on the passage, "How different, how dreadfully different are the judgments of God!" (*Waiting Father*, 46). In this respect, the story is reminiscent of Jesus' appraisal of the poor widow in Luke 21:1–4, whose meager offering is greater than all the others. Such is the undoing and reversal of everything we call "great" in the new age that is dawning.

If this parable (16:19–31) has an Egyptian progenitor, by the last few verses it has been thoroughly Christianized. In ancient tales it is not uncommon for the living and the dead to communicate through the veil, much as the rich man in the underworld asks favors of Father Abraham in paradise. But in the dialogue that follows, Abraham patiently explains the necessity of faith in Israel's Scripture, to which the rich man objects, "No, father Abraham; but if someone goes to them from the dead, they will repent." Abraham is given the best, last, and most explicitly Christian line in the story:

108

"If they do not listen to Moses and the prophets, neither will they be convinced even if someone rises from the dead."

The fourth among Lukan classics—following the Good Samaritan, the Prodigal Son, and Lazarus and the Rich Man—is the parable of the Pharisee and the Tax Collector (Luke 18:9–14). Although it is not as complex as the other three, it raises a literary question with decidedly theological implications: Is it a true parable or an example story? That is, does it metaphorically embody the antithesis of grace and works righteousness, or does it offer an example of how to pray and how not to pray? The difficulty of the question is illustrated by the range of opinions among interpreters. Jeremias (*Parables of Jesus*, 139–44) places it in his chapter on "God's Mercy for Sinners," while Arland Hultgren (*Parables of Jesus*, 118–28) considers it under "Parables of Exemplary Behavior." The parable fits—and stretches—both categories. Luke himself frames it as a parable about two kinds of righteousness. It begins when two extreme "types" of people enter the temple with very different kinds of motives: one enters to feel small before God, the other to puff himself up. The two address God with quite different sorts of prayer. Of the two, it is no surprise that one is a Pharisee, a member of the most observant of Jewish parties. The second man, however, has more in common with the Dishonest Steward than his distinguished fellow worshiper: like the steward, he makes his living by taking a healthy commission from the taxes he extorts from his countrymen. Three chapters earlier it was the Pharisees who grumbled that Jesus is associating with tax collectors: "This fellow welcomes sinners and eats with them" (Luke 15:2). The scene is set. Luke's ability to create a cameo of the kingdom is nowhere shown to greater effect.

The Pharisee rehearses his good points, whose luster depends on a comparison with the failings of others. His self-righteousness is so bad it is funny. The portrait reads as a caricature of Pharisaism, for as David Flusser argues, the Judaism of Jesus' day had moderated the black-and-white severity of the contrast between the righteous and the wicked, especially as found in the Psalms, in favor of a more relativistic understanding of human foibles. "Indeed, the prayers of this spiritual climate bear out that it was inconceivable to present oneself to God as meriting attention and consideration for being good, or righteous, or virtuous, or just—for these qualities are attributes that belong only to God" ("A New Sensitivity," 118–19). The stereotype serves Luke's purpose, however, which is to lead the reader to another mode of self-evaluation, to a better way of praying, and ultimately to a new understanding of God. The tax collector's prayer does not draw on his moral achievements, since he apparently has none, and makes no reference to anything but his own sinful life. After such an honest reckoning, the only possible prayer can be a prayer for mercy.

There are many surprises in this vignette: a tax collector in the temple—and praying, no less; a Pharisee pilloried in an unprecedented way. But the biggest surprise of all is that the tax collector, and not the Pharisee, leaves "church" in possession of God's righteousness. He has been acquitted. Like most biblical writers, Luke is not much interested in the psychology of religion. If he were, he would have sketched out the Pharisee's nagging sense of emptiness even as he flawlessly performs his religious tasks, and he would have dwelled on the sense of assurance that warms the heart of the forgiven sinner. But he does none of that. All he wishes to do is to capture the *difference* between two types of righteousness and to do so in bold relief, as in a medieval morality play.

The parable of the Pharisee and the Tax Collector is part example story and part parable. It clearly teaches us what true prayer looks like in the kingdom of God: it is not *that*, it is *this*. Luke frames it, however, not as a story about prayer but about the sort of righteousness that characterizes those in the kingdom. Each man addresses "God" by name one time. But for the Pharisee, that "God" is an idol and a figment of his religious imagination. For the tax collector, however, "God" is the true God and the only source of mercy for all who seek it. Thus the story does not merely exemplify actions and attitudes *in* the kingdom, though it does do that, but it also reveals the divine reversal of all human rules and norms of righteousness. Because it is ultimately about God, it is a true parable *of* the kingdom. Once again, the Teller of the tale makes all the difference. Without the ministry and impending death of Jesus, we have a stale vignette of two kinds of people and two sorts of religious behavior. But reading with Luke yields much more. For in the context of Jesus' love for the poor, the outcast, and sinners, this little story glows with insight and hope.

110

Perhaps it is inevitable that reading "with" the three evangelists would emphasize the distinctiveness of their respective theological tendencies. As I predicted at the beginning of the chapter, Mark is brief and eschatological; Matthew is ecclesial, didactic, and allegorical; Luke is literary and universal. These broad distinctions remain as markers of their theopoetic genius. Elsewhere (in chapter 1), I have suggested that the occasional character of the parables and the theological diversity of the Gospels do not allow us to view the Jesus story as a "grand narrative." This is the place to make the alternative claim, namely, that despite the diversity of stories *about* Jesus and the various nuances of detail in the stories Jesus told, there is such a thing as the Christian story *of* Jesus. While it is always good homiletical advice to "preach Luke's or Matthew's or Mark's narrative" and to avoid the mistake of harmonization, it is even more important to preach *Jesus* crucified and risen from the dead. A church in Winston-Salem, North Carolina, has some good advice embossed on the inside of the pulpit, where it is visible only to the preacher. It is a quotation from John 12:21: "We wish to see Jesus." In our rush to acknowledge the postmodern condition (with the center not holding and all that), it is easy to overlook the theological and aesthetic coherence of the Gospels. They may not read as a single Grand Narrative, but the many differences among them achieve a higher unity in the single figure of Jesus, whose character, mission, and destiny remain remarkably the same in the several literary witnesses to him. Together, the Gospels' portrait of Jesus is sufficiently thick and real as to render a figure who *was* a historical person and *is* a life-giving presence among us (see Lischer, *End of Words*, 123–26).

Often it is the poets who recognize the correspondence between the biblical portraits of Jesus and their later replications in human experience. While historians and exegetes ask, "Did it happen?" or "Did he really say that?" it is the artist who admonishes us, "You've got great material. Trust it! Preach it!"

CHAPTER 4

Reading the Parables
in the Human Condition

The parables of Jesus are human documents. They chronicle the crises, conflicts, disappointments, dead ends, and joyous new beginnings common to us all. They not only shed light on Jesus and the kingdom he proclaimed but because they are profoundly true to human nature and experience, they have generated echoes and reflections among literary practitioners of succeeding ages. In an earlier chapter we noted something of the history of biblical and rabbinic storytelling that lies *behind* the parables of Jesus. In this chapter we will explore the generative nature of these same parables, which is the *future* they continue to create in every generation of readers and writers. It is in this context that critic Robert Funk speaks of Jesus as *precursor* to the artistic visions of many. By this, Funk means more than ongoing and future performances of the New Testament script. We have seen this phenomenon most prominently in music, art, drama, and modern fiction. One thinks, most recently, of the Prodigal Son theme that runs through Marilynne Robinson's novels *Gilead* and *Home*. Funk understands Jesus as the poet and theological artisan whose *language* somehow creates the vision of the poets who have come after him (*Jesus as Precursor*, 152; cf. Schneiders, *Revelatory Text*, 149–50). By reading the parables in the light of modern and secular parabolic writings, we cannot help but gain in understanding of Jesus, the precursor. And reading Kierkegaard and Kafka in conversation with Jesus'

113

parables will yield new angles of appreciation for their artistic and religious power.

Derangements

At the very beginning of Ray Bradbury's classic science fiction novel *Fahrenheit 451*, the reader experiences a disquieting reversal of expectations. In the world of a future totalitarian society, the role of the firefighter has changed dramatically. No longer the respected guardian of life and property, the firefighter is now devoted to the burning of books and homes with books in them. One of the characters innocently asks, "Is it true that long ago firemen put fires *out* instead of going to start them?" (8). In some of the parables the same sort of perceptual displacement occurs: what is plausible becomes implausible, role reversals occur, and accepted values are turned upside down. A speck of leaven, which carries universally negative associations in Judaism, including Paul, is given a positive value in one of Jesus' parables. An impoverished widow and a beggar become signs of God's favor. A Pharisee is rejected, a Samaritan is praised, an owner winks at chicanery, and a crook turns out to be a hero. What is going on here?

Classical literature drew upon an enormous inventory of *topoi* (Greek for "commonplaces," traditional themes or formulas), moral and cultural "scripts" that anchored an entire civilization's thinking about a comprehensive range of topics. The topoi combine an image with a thematic action. The graciousness of a hospitable host, for example, or the unexpected appearance of wisdom in a young warrior—all served as indispensible topoi for the ancient poets (Scholes and Kellogg, *Nature of Narrative*, 17–56; cf. Ong, *Orality and Literacy*, 57–68). The key to the topoi was their dependability. In his parables it was precisely that quality, the solidity of the anchors themselves, that Jesus was willing to upend.

Take the figure of the judge, long a symbol for God in the religion of Israel. In Luke 18:1–8 Jesus tells a story in which a judge "neither feared God nor had respect for people." His life is a photographic negative of the summary of the law in Luke 10: love of God and love of neighbor. He has no regard for either, and he admits such in a characteristically Lukan interior monologue. Although he occupies an exalted position in Jewish society, this judge's inner

114

attitude and outward actions represent violations of role. He lives in a world whose justice is so unlike God's that the very symbol of God's righteousness is completely perverted. The poor widow lives in the same ugly world, and all she wants from it is "justice." Her only recourse is to hassle the judge night and day, wearing him out with her "continual coming" until he relents. Tradition knows this story by two titles: the parable of the Importunate Widow or the parable of the Unjust Judge. They are costars in the parable, and both are given dialogue, but the figure of the judge controls the story. He resolves to grant the widow's request not because he has had a change of heart or has decided to live up to the virtues inherent in his office, but because he wants to get her off his back. To which Jesus adds, "Listen to what the unjust judge says."

This is the world in which the followers of Jesus must live and make their witness to the kingdom of God. In such a world it is necessary to pray and not lose heart. The reader might have expected a positive analogy between God and the earthly judge, much in the way Luke compares God to a searching housewife, a gracious host, or a loving father. But in this parable, the object of prayer is the divine being identified only as "God"—not "your heavenly Father"—and this chilly divinity is not given the warmth of a human face. The parable turns on the absence of God in the world. Jesus' followers will serve God in a world from which the comforting evidences of the sacred are missing. The disciples will live, work, and suffer, as Bonhoeffer predicted, *"etsi deus non daretur*—as if God did not exist—but always in the presence of God. Even in such a world, the obedience of prayer is always possible, and God will not delay in answering.

Luke introduces the parable as an exhortation to pray always and not to lose heart. Only by its conclusion do we realize that the widow's prayer is a parable within a parable, for her persistent request for justice is itself a parable of a larger and more profound request: Christians are, or should be, praying incessantly for the Parousia, the ultimate vindication of God's justice. In Luke 17:20 the Pharisees (of all people) want to know "when the kingdom of God is coming." Jesus gives them a brief answer, but then turns to his disciples with a more extensive set of instructions. The clue to the eschatological nature of the parable occurs in a verb that betrays Christian anxiety over the second coming: "Will he *delay* long in helping them?" (18:7). By this the reader is alerted to the

115

Lord's final question: "When the Son of Man comes, will he find faith on earth?" (18:8). The parable begins as a story told by Jesus; it ends with a mysterious reference to the Son of Man, which I understand as the time-transcendent name Jesus adopted from the tradition and applied to himself. The point of Jesus' final question is not, "Will the Son of Man ever return?" His question has more to do with human endurance than divine faithfulness: Not "Will God come?" but "Will you keep praying? Or will the godlessness of the world so crush you that when the Son of Man does return, all he will find is a dead world, frozen in unbelief?"

The grim and joyless world of the widow and the judge reappears again and again in the parables of Franz Kafka. Although descended from prominent rabbis, Kafka was not a religious person. Indeed, his fictional world is so empty of God that God's very absence functions as a character or, at the least, a palpable condition of modern life. Christians read his parables because in their form and pacing, among all the secular successors of Jesus, they most closely replicate the "feel" of the Lord's parables, but with no kingdom and no joy. Paul neatly summarizes Kafka's universe: "aliens . . . and strangers, . . . having no hope and without God in the world" (Eph. 2:12). If Jesus' parables are photographs of the kingdom of God, Kafka's are their negative.

A second reason for reading Kafka is the prophetic character of his writing. As a Jew, an artist, and a terminally ill person—he died of tuberculosis in 1924 at the age of 40—Kafka was the thrice-estranged Prophet of Alienation in the modern era. His parables are harbingers of the banal, bureaucratic, meaningless, and increasingly totalitarian experience of millions in the twentieth century. He himself worked anonymously for a large insurance company in his native city of Prague. In the coming decades, 90,000 Jews would disappear from the same city, transforming the vibrant synagogues of Prague into museums; three of his sisters would die in concentration camps during the war. His characters are often punished, but they never know why or understand what Erich Heller calls the "fearful disproportion of guilt and punishment" (introduction, *Basic Kafka*, xix). He wrote a bitter "Letter" to his domineering father, in which he dreamed, "We might both have found each other in Judaism," but it was not to be ("Letter," *Basic Kafka*, 215). "Kafkaesque" remains the shorthand expression for everything in the modern era that baffles and thwarts the human spirit.

116

We do not read Jesus and Kafka together simply because the latter is so perfect a negative to the gospel's positive. There is something in *Jesus* too about the lost and banal existence of those outside his Father's reign that finds its way into Kafka. Of course, it comes by way of Kafka's own experience, but whatever it is, it shows Jesus not only to be a preacher of the kingdom of God but also a diagnostician of the human predicament before God. It makes him Precursor to Kafka. Two stylistic considerations confirm this judgment: one is the "flat" characterization in both storytellers. A second is the spare realism with which they both tell their stories.

The critic and interpreter of Kafka, Walter Benjamin, decreed, "There is nothing that commends a story to memory more effectively than that chaste compactness which precludes psychological analysis." Why is this important? Because, the more completely psychological motivation is ruled out, "the greater becomes the story's claim to a place in the memory of the listener, the more completely is it integrated into his own experience, the greater will be his inclination to repeat it to someone else someday, sooner or later" (*Illuminations*, 91). The Bible famously avoids psychological explanation of its characters' behavior. Rarely does it explain a character's action from the inside out. We never hear a biblical actor ask the director, "What's my motivation?" This is in keeping with the Hebrew use of *parataxis*, the narrative technique that takes its power from the juxtaposition of events, not the explanation of them. The story of David and Bathsheba is illustrative. Its drama moves from event to event without providing a single window into the characters' interior life: "So David sent messengers to get her, and she came to him, and he lay with her. . . . Then she returned to her house" (2 Sam. 11:4). Throughout the story the actions and the dialogue are powerful but emotionally blunted. If there is any soul-searching that occurs, it is manifest only at the end of the tragedy in regret and loud repentance.

The Gospels also exclude the interior examination of its characters in favor of the acts that signify and serve the reign of God. The Synoptics dart from event to event, often with a minimal narrative thread and with no attempt to explain Jesus' motives by means of spoken soliloquies or interior monologues (the Fourth Gospel is another story). We have nothing in the Synoptics like Homer's repeated disclosures of Odysseus's inner debates: "deeply moved he spoke to his own mighty heart" (four times in *Odyssey* 5; quoted

117

in Scholes and Kellogg, *Nature of Narrative*, 182). Why this is the case with Jesus is not hard to understand; for who can know the thoughts of God's own Son? When Homer and later classics provide lengthy and articulate accounts of their heroes' inner musings, they are not indulging in psychology or stream-of-consciousness narration that pretends to mimic raw mental processes. That would come much later in the history of literature. They are practicing rhetoric and following the standards of eloquence common to their age (Scholes and Kellogg, *Nature of Narrative*, 182–85). Similarly, the few soliloquies or interior monologues in the parables of Jesus are not marked by the sometimes chaotic processes of the brain, but by attention to rhetoric. The Prodigal does not let out a cry when he sees his father; he has prepared a *speech*. Even when the Dishonest Steward finds his life unraveling, he delivers his interior monologue in a carefully constructed parallel antithesis: "to dig I am not able, to beg I am ashamed" (Luke 16:3, lit.).

The modern literary temper favors *syntaxis*, the historical, psychological, and grammatical devices that help the reader connect the dots between motive and action. The parables of Jesus and Kafka are notable for the absence of the very explanations we crave: How does the Prodigal *feel* about his older brother? Why did he leave home in the first place? Why would anyone contaminate a neighbor's wheat field? What goes through the Rich Man's mind as he steps over Lazarus every day? Why didn't the priest or the Levite stop to help? The parables of Jesus and Kafka do not get bogged down in such questions. Their characters are stock figures representing a variety of roles in the village, city, or synagogue; their presence only facilitates the actions and reactions of the plot. They are either stereotypes like the Unjust Judge or the Pharisee and the Tax Collector, or, as in the stories of Luke and Kafka, they are anonymous human beings, whose very namelessness enhances their representative identity as Everyman. In Luke it is "a certain man" (*anthropos tis*, 15:11); Kafka's protagonists are sometimes designated by initial only. And yet the starkness of these representative characters and simple plots replicates something in *us* in a way that eludes psychological explanation.

Closely related to these observations on character is the spare realism evident in the parables of Jesus and Kafka. If this seems a contradiction, it is because the parables of both are devoid of the attributes our contemporary culture would consider "realistic,"

118

namely, psychological motivation, descriptive passages, or a specific sense of geographical place and time. Absent these characteristics, the parables' vaunted realism comes closer to what Klyne Snodgrass refers to as "staged portraits of reality" (*Stories with Intent*, 15). The realistic parables of Jesus and Kafka are evocations of life as it is lived, but they are carefully trimmed and disciplined in order to craft an effect that goes beyond the reader's admiration of "realistic writing." What remains is a brute factuality about the human condition, one that appears to have been achieved by subtracting any embellishment or detail that would separate the reality depicted in the parable from that of the reader. The painter Georgia O'Keeffe has this to say about realism: "Nothing is less real than realism. . . . Details are confusing. It is only by selection, by elimination, by emphasis, that we get at the real meaning of things" (Georgia O'Keeffe Museum, Santa Fe, New Mexico).

In Kafka's parable "Give It Up!" an unnamed man hurries down a deserted, unnamed street in an unnamed city. When he compares his watch with the tower clock in town, he realizes that the hour is much later than he thought. The shock of this discovery makes him uncertain of the way. Fortunately, he sees a policeman and runs to him to ask the way. But the policeman replies, "You asking me the way?" . . . "Give it up!"

We may think of this parable in relation to the Unjust Judge. Both stories are set in a world filled with futility. A judge is supposed to care about justice; a policeman's role is to help those in need. In both parables the hour is late, and in Kafka's the reader suspects that what the man really wants is for the times to be set right. Neither authority figure shows the least bit of concern for the one in need of help. But in Kafka's parable, the last act is missing: there is no recourse to a being who transcends the futility of the situation. In Jesus' parable, the widow will gain her justice; in Kafka's parable, the policeman only laughs and repeats himself: "Give it up!" (*Basic Kafka*, 157–58).

Another, more explicit, derangement of role occurs in the figure of God in the parable of the Dishonest Steward in Luke 16. In the master's commendation of the steward's behavior, the Old Testament God of righteousness has devolved into another sort of character. Verse 8 reads, "The master [*ho kyrios*] commended the dishonest steward for his shrewdness" (RSV). Considering the steward's shady behavior and the rectitude usually associated with "the master," the reader is jarred by the latter's moral laxity, especially in a Gospel in which the Lord figure is not unwilling to exclude evildoers from the kingdom (Luke 13:22–30).

In most of Kafka's parables, like those of Jesus, the actual figure of God does not appear. Kafka makes an exception in a parable called "Poseidon." If the Unjust Judge or the Dishonest Steward makes us wonder if God always plays fair with our lives, Kafka's raises another concern. It is more in keeping with the modern suspicion that, even if there is a God, such a God is remote and disconnected from our daily concerns. In fact, Kafka's God has his own problems. The parable purports to chronicle an average day in the life of God. It begins, "Poseidon sat at his desk, doing figures. The administration of all the waters gave him endless work." The God who thunders over Sinai, delivers Israel from captivity, and intervenes in the lives of ordinary people is, in Kafka's world, a glorified clerk who is bored with his job. "What irritated him most . . . was to hear of the conceptions formed about him: how he was always riding about through the tides with his trident. When all the while he sat here in the depths of the world-ocean, doing figures uninterruptedly." The God of Jesus' parables is the God who seeks laborers for his vineyard, who searches for the lost, and rejoices when they are found. Kafka's God, Poseidon, is waiting for the fall of the world when "he would be able to make a quick little tour" (*Basic Kafka*, 153–54).

A similar view of the "the gods" is found in Kierkegaard. In his parable "The Boredom of the Gods," the gods communicate their boredom to Adam and through him to the whole human race. "Then the population of the world increased, and the peoples were bored *en masse*." The parable attributes humankind's decision to build the Tower of Babel not to rebellion against the gods but to the sin of lethargy (*Parables*, 11). Not every sin represents a grand rebellion on the order of Satan's offense in *Paradise Lost*. The boredom of the gods in Kierkegaard prepares the way for Kafka's notion of the banality of evil, which in Jesus' parables is represented by the mediocrity of the servant who buries his talent in the ground, or the meanness of the slave who refuses to forgive even the smallest debt.

A longer and more complex derangement of expectations also occurs in the parable of the Good Samaritan. Before we read the Good Samaritan with the "saints" in chapter 6 (below), let us consider a modern literary appraisal of the parable. In his article "The Good Samaritan as Metaphor," Robert Funk argues that the

120

parable is neither an allegory nor an example story but an extended metaphor, that is, a "true parable." What links Funk's reading with the medieval tradition and modern theological exegesis is that his conclusions rest on the literary *genre* of the story. A piece of literature cannot be interpreted until we know what it *is*. For example, it takes only seconds to recognize the genre of a joke. "A priest, a rabbi, and a used car salesman walk into a bar. . . ." We know immediately how we are meant to respond. When Jesus begins a story, "A man had two sons . . . ," it is the same. We do not expect him to give their names and addresses. If we judge the story to be an allegory, we expect it will yield many truths; if it is an example story, we are prepared to learn a lesson.

The parable of the Good Samaritan, says Funk, is a metaphor. The first three sentences introduce us to three characters: a man, a priest, and a Levite. It is a realistic story whose action and characters are so recognizable that that it immediately creates expectations in the listener, then violates them. The reader's response *makes* the story work. Even though the character of the Samaritan occupies the entire second half of the story, the reader has already identified with the Jew who fell among thieves. It is a dangerous road. Muggings happen all the time. Since our religious leaders have shown themselves indifferent to our needs, no doubt the one who stops will be a Jewish layman.

It is the fourth sentence of the parable, the one introduced with "but," that deranges our expectations: "But a Samaritan . . ." (Luke 10:33). If we read this parable with the sensibilities of a Jew, we will read it in solidarity with the victim. Through his swollen eyes we will watch the priest and the Levite pass by until, with a combination of horror and hope, we will look up to see our enemy bend over us and, with unexpected compassion, care for us.

There is nothing about the victim, the Samaritan, the inn, the innkeeper, or any of the other features of the parable that suggests ecclesiastical or dogmatic truths. Nevertheless, the stuff of the *vehicle*—the story's images, action, and characters—cries out for a *tenor*, or theological idea. But it is not a meaning found in the precise identification of the story with the church's teachings. The meaning is *evoked* in the readers' experience of the story itself and in the manner by which it resonates with its hearers' lives.

That *evocation*, as opposed to *designation*, is the work of metaphor. C. S. Lewis helps us understand the difference when he

121

distinguishes between a Master's Metaphor and a Pupil's Metaphor. A master's metaphor is substitutionary. The master already has a firm grasp of the idea he intends to teach the student and, like the allegorist, dutifully imparts that knowledge by means of the strategies drawn from any number of pictures at his disposal. In preaching, a master's metaphor is a sermon illustration. In the master's metaphor the vehicle (or image) is clearly subservient to the tenor (idea). From the perspective of the pupil, however, learning takes place by immersion in an experience without categories or preconceptions. In preaching, the pupil's metaphor is a true metaphor; it carries with it infinitely more power because it is the *only* way a particular truth may express itself ("Bluspels and Flalansferes," in *Rehabilitations*, 144–46). For example, one may learn about French Impressionism by attending a lecture on the subject and only later visiting a museum, or one can walk into a museum and confront the world of Impressionism through the lens of Monet's *Water Lilies* (for what follows, Lischer, "Role of Metaphor," 282–84).

Much of the history of theology is a history of controversy over the status of the church's metaphors. Is "God the Father" a master's metaphor or a pupil's metaphor? If it is the former, other metaphors may be selected to convey what was originally meant by the expression. If it is the latter, "God the Father" is not merely illustrative of the being and disposition of God but is indispensable to the affirmation of God's relationship to Jesus and, therefore, to the believer's experience of God.

To cite another example, behind the freely created metaphors for "atonement," we do not find nonmetaphoric expressions of dogma. Such words as "expiation" and "justification" first worked as pupil's metaphors because they necessitated startling juxtapositions of ancient images of the mercy seat or the divine court with the execution of a particular person named Jesus. All the formative metaphors of Christian theology were pupil's metaphors, for they gave expression to that for which there was no preexisting idea. Before the proclamation of the gospel, there was no neutral concept of "incarnation" or "reconciliation" for which the writer might substitute another illustration for the sake of vividness. The gospel is the decisive break with a purely substitutionary theory of metaphor that reduces the good news to an illustration of a greater truth.

122

Even the most startling of pupil's metaphors have had a way of calcifying into propositions and concepts. This has been the fate of the Good Samaritan. But if we interpret the parable with the fresh eyes of a pupil, we will read it with a view from the ditch. In the process of identifying with the victim, we will cycle through the stages of metaphoric response: we will be serially dismayed, puzzled, surprised, and restored by the actions of the outsider, for the parable suggests that our deliverance, too, will come to us from a direction we least expect. Funk does not identify the Samaritan with Jesus, as does a majority of the interpretative tradition, but simply concludes, "In the kingdom mercy is always a surprise."

In Funk's reading of the Good Samaritan, the power of the parable lies in the offensive identity of the rescuer. Similarly, in Kierkegaard's parable of "The Happy Conflagration," the audience to a circus cannot tolerate the identity of the one sent to save them:

> It happened that a fire broke out backstage in a theater. The clown came out to inform the public. They thought it was just a jest and applauded. He repeated his warning, they shouted even louder. So I think the world will come to an end amid general applause from all the wits, who believe that it is a joke.
>
> (*Parables*, 3)

A similar theme emerges in another parable by Kierkegaard and in one of Jesus' parable-like sayings. One might title both these parables "Telling the Truth Is a Sure Way to Make Them Think You Are Crazy." In Kierkegaard's parable "Bang, the Earth Is Round," a man escapes from a mental institution and, in order not to be apprehended, vows only to speak the objective truth. In that way, everyone will be convinced that he is sane. He picks up a ball, which reminds him of an unassailable truth, and therefore everywhere he goes he says, "Bang, the earth is round." He is quickly returned to the hospital for further treatment (*Parables*, 50).

In Matthew 11:16–19 Jesus reflects on the same problem by means of a similitude, comparing his generation to children playing a game of "Funerals" in the marketplace:

> We played the flute for you,
>   and you did not dance;
> We wailed,
>   and you did not mourn.
>   (v. 17)

123

John the Baptist came fasting, and they said he had a demon. The Son of Man came eating and drinking, and he was accused of being a glutton and a drunkard. Both John and Jesus did the expected thing, and both were reviled and rejected. In all three Synoptic Gospels, Jesus' demonstration of power over demons induces his opponents to charge him with demon possession. In the Gospel of Mark, his ministry of healing is so powerful that his family attempts to restrain him, for the people are saying, "He has gone out of his mind" (Mark 3:21).

The story of the Widow's Mite is not the sort of "derangement" we have been discussing, but it does represent an inversion of expectations. Nor is it a parable proper, but in its highly visual contrast of the poor widow with "the rich people" and the portrayal of her insignificance against the massive temple buildings, it functions parabolically as an object lesson within Luke's general discussion of wealth and discipleship. In Kierkegaard's parable "The Swindler and the Widow's Mite," the widow has wrapped her two pennies in a little cloth before she goes up to the temple to make her offering. A flimflam artist tricks her into exchanging her cloth for an empty one, with the result that, unbeknownst to her, she places an empty cloth into the treasury. "I wonder if Christ would not still have said what he said of her, that 'she gave more than all the rich?'" (*Parables*, 36). It is a rhetorical question whose implied answer is clearly yes. It is a true question in that the reader is held accountable to the parable and is obligated to make a similar life-response.

The Surreal

The allegory of the Great Feast in Matthew 22 tells the story of a king's reaction when his invitations to his son's wedding are spurned. We have already discussed how differently Luke and Matthew treat the material received from a common source. By the end of Matthew's version, the king instructs his slaves to invite everyone to his banquet, so that the wedding hall is filled with guests. To this allegory only Matthew appends a parable (22:11–14). The reader must imagine the drama of an oral performance of this story. The storyteller pauses and allows his silence to re-create the stunned silence in the hall as the king enters. This is the moment of truth. He looks around at the guests, and his eye falls on a man who has not donned the traditional "wedding robe" (v. 11). He has come to the party improperly dressed. Is this merely a faux pas, or does it represent a deeper disjunction between the flawed nature of the guest and the sacred nature of the banquet, one that is captured by the universal symbol of shame and humiliation—the wrong clothes? In the garden of Eden, God asks Adam a sartorial question: "Who told you that you were naked?" (Gen. 3:11). In Genesis (3:21–24), God casts Adam and Eve not into outer darkness but into the world, but not before re-dressing them with a garment of God's own making. In Matthew 22:12–14, the man without a robe does not fare so well. "Friend," the king says ominously, "how did you get in here without a wedding robe?" The man might have replied, "O King, I did not crash the party. I was invited. I was among those whom your slaves 'gathered' in the wedding hall." But he was speechless. The king has him thrown into "outer darkness." To which Jesus (or Matthew) adds, "For many are called, but few are chosen."

Of all Jesus' parables, the parable of the Wedding Garment is the only one that qualifies as surreal. Among the many paradoxical stories told by Jesus, this one stands alone as eerily and blatantly irrational. The guest was *invited*. The invitation itself bespeaks a certain graciousness on the part of the king, who orders his agents to sweep the streets and to gather all whom they find. They gathered "both good and bad," to be sure, but everything we know about Matthew leads us to believe that the invitation of God, like the call of Matthew himself, wipes a bad slate clean.

That brings us to Kafka.

In his parable "Before the Law," a man from the country comes to a great palace to seek admittance to "the Law." At the door stands a fierce guard, who does not allow him to enter. Behind him, at innumerable other doors, stand other sentries. Somewhere in that great building resides the Law, but how to get to it? "The Law, he thinks, should be accessible to every man at all times." Patiently the man decides to wait, first days, and then years, but to no avail. He even gets to know the fleas in the doorkeeper's fur collar and begs the very fleas to help him persuade the guard. The man grows old, and just before he dies, he imagines that he sees a brilliant radiance streaming from the door of the Law. On the brink of revelation, the man says, "'Everyone strives to attain the Law. . . . How does it come about, then, that in all these years no one has come seeking admittance but me?' . . . The guard replies, 'No one but you could gain

125

admittance through this door, since this door was intended only for you. I am now going to shut it'" (*Basic Kafka*, 176). All that is lacking is the phrase "Many are called, but few are chosen" (Matt. 22:14).

Kafka's parable has surface resonances with Lazarus and the Rich Man. Both men waste away as they wait interminably, with no results. Both are positioned outside a place of well-being, and both are so bereft of human care that they are befriended by lower creatures, dogs and fleas. But it is the paradox of call and rejection that links Kafka's parable to the Wedding Garment. Both men are irrevocably lost. They do not suffer collateral losses, disappointments, or temporary setbacks. In the world of parable, to be lost is to lose the very thing you were meant to have or to be. In Matthew, the tragedy is that, although this man was among the many called to salvation, he is disqualified from the blessing that had his name written on it. The same is true for the man in Kafka's parable: the door intended only for him is closed forever.

But why? It is a trademark of Kafka's fiction that no reason or clue is ever given for the loss. In Matthew the "reason," if we may call it that, centers in the lack of a wedding garment. Interpreters have not been slow to demystify the garment by exchanging its metaphorical suggestiveness for allegorical specificity: the guest lacked true discipleship; he refused the clothing of Christ's righteousness; he failed to "put on" the Lord Jesus and instead made provision for the flesh; he was not baptized. Every explanation of the garment, however, is imported from other parts of Matthew or from Paul or the larger tradition. None belongs to the parable. Deeper than the explanatory tags is a more frightening reality. It is possible to lose the very best thing that has ever been given to you, which for the Jew is life in the light of Torah, and for the Christian the grace of the everlasting banquet.

Occlusions

Kafka's classic masterpiece "The Metamorphosis" tells the story of how Gregor Samsa's life changed after he was turned into an enormous insect. One of its most touching episodes occurs when the insect crawls from his hiding place and moves toward the living room, drawn by the sounds of his sister's violin playing. "Was he an animal, that music had such an effect upon him? He felt as if the way were opening before him to the unknown nourishment he craved" (*Basic Kafka*, 44–45). Despite the loneliness of his characters in an alien world, many of them sense the reality of something better and more fulfilling. One of Kafka's great themes is his characters' desire for communion with "the source of unknown nourishment"—and the many obstacles that make that impossible. It is significant that his famous "Letter to His Father," in which he finally clarified his feelings for his overbearing father, was never delivered. Two of his parables illustrate this theme.

In "An Imperial Message," the emperor is dying. He has chosen "you, his humble subject," to convey his message to his vast number of subjects. The messenger departs, bearing the image of the sun on his breast, but his path is occluded by the sheer crush of humanity surrounding him—and he has yet to emerge from the corridors and innumerable courts of the palace itself. Even if he were to find his way out of the palace, the imperial capital would lie before him, "crammed to bursting with its own sediment." No one could possibly get through, even with a message from the emperor. "But you sit at your window when evening falls and dream it to yourself" (*Basic Kafka*, 159–60).

The second parable is "The Bucket Rider." A poor man is in dire need of coal to warm his house. He will make his appeal to the coal dealer, who has already proved deaf to ordinary appeals for help. The poor man is so cold and his bucket so empty that he can fly on his bucket to the coal dealer's house. When he arrives on his bucket, he cries out to the coal dealer, but to no avail. The coal dealer is old, partially deaf, and senile. "Do I hear rightly," he asks his wife, "a customer?" "It must be an old, a very old customer, that can move me so deeply." With motiveless malignity the wife assures him he is hearing things. There is no one there, she insists. The coal dealer reminds his wife that they have endless supplies of coal, but she dismisses the idea. The poor man promises to pay for even one shovelful of coal, "but not just now." With a wave of her apron, she dispatches the man to the regions of ice, where he is lost forever (*Basic Kafka*, 149–51).

Many of Jesus' parables feature a journey, a search, or a task in which the person sent or appointed then encounters an obstacle. The way to completion is blocked or occluded. The ordinary actions of daily living meet with unexpected interferences and produce intractable conflicts. A man sows his field with wheat, and an enemy

127

pollutes it with darnel. A slave with much to be thankful for refuses to forgive a pittance to his fellow slave, who may be able to pay one day, "but not just now." An employer is generous to his workers, and a father forgives his son, but both acts of grace produce only resentment. Like the Bucket Rider, the man without a proper garment goes to the right place for help but is cast into outer darkness. Five improvident bridesmaids are locked out of the banquet by the very Bridegroom they have been waiting for. A rich man with an excellent view of heaven spends his eternity in hell. Augustine once remarked, "Do not despair, one thief was saved. Do not presume, one thief was lost." These occlusions in the parables of Jesus are powerful and real. The enemies of God's rule will try by any means possible to impede the purposes of God on earth, and they will succeed. The ultimate badge of their success is the vineyard owner's son, sent to reclaim what is rightfully his, who is put to a cruel death and whose body is tossed over the wall.

In the Gospels these occlusions ultimately fail; the badge of their failure is the resurrection of the Son from the dead. His victory is signified in the Scripture:

> The stone that the builders rejected
>   has become the cornerstone;
> this was the Lord's doing,
>   and it is amazing in our eyes.
>   (Mark 12:10–11)

In comparing the obstacles presented in Jesus' parables with the occlusions and dead ends in Kafka, it is important to remember that Jesus did not live in a world of meaninglessness, angst, and alienation. In his parables, the way to God's kingdom is more often blocked by active rebellion than existential ennui or a mysterious absence of the good. From the foundation of the world, humankind has disobeyed the Creator and deified itself. Luther vividly depicts original sin as "the proneness toward evil; the loathing of the good; the disdain for light and wisdom but fondness for darkness" (*Romans*, 167–68). So also in Jesus' parables, the child is capable of saying "No!" to the father. Apart from the drag of stupidity and resentment in some of the actors in Jesus' parables, the actions of most of his sinful characters are willful *acts* of cruelty and violence, like those of the Wicked Tenants or the Unforgiving Servant. They

128

mirror the same sort of wickedness that will be unleashed upon Jesus himself in the larger Gospel narrative.

The occlusions that occur in Kafka are not characterized by rebellion and disobedience. They more closely resemble exquisite forms of suffocation. It is a tribute to his genius that in being absorbed into the world of his novels and stories, readers feel that they too are about to suffocate. Kafka does not doubt that real sins lie at the core of modern estrangement, but they are so primordial or finely diffused among the faceless powers that rule our lives that they cannot be named, repented, or defied. As Freud, Foucault, and others have argued, the powers of our civilization are so deeply and massively hidden that we experience them as an unhappy residue or a default condition, be it anxiety, estrangement, or guilt.

Against the many occlusions in the ancient and modern world, only one figure succeeds in delivering the Imperial Message. In the story of Jesus, the breakthrough to "the source of unknown nourishment" occurs. The genius of the parables is that they not only reflect the real obstacles to fulfillment, but they also encapsulate God's breakthrough in poetic terms. Indeed, the parables of Jesus *are* the Imperial Message writ small, and those who are sent to tell his stories are messengers with the image of the Son on their chest.

Kafka implies that the religious believer can only dream that God is capable of transmitting a message through the suffocating world and the occluded human heart. But in Jesus, the dream comes true. Its partial fulfillment occurs when the distant realm is brought near in the ministry, defeat, and victory of the messenger himself. For now, the kingdom's only mode is crisis, and one catches a glimpse of it only in the fragmented opportunities of ordinary life: the generosity of the employer, the love of the father for both sons, the master's forgiveness—all these are poetic intimations of the Great Arrival of God's grace, on the day when,

> The crooked shall be made straight,
> and the rough places plain:
> And the glory of the Lord shall be revealed,
> and all flesh shall see it together.
> (Isa. 40:4–5 KJV)

CHAPTER 5

Reading the Parables
with the Poor

In our town the authorities are trying to devise a safer and more humane way for the growing pool of the unemployed to find daily work.

> Day laborers, many of them Latino, gather at the corner of Jones Ferry and Davie roads to wait to be picked up for construction work, and community members have been trying to find a location for an official center where workers could be protected from wage theft and benefit from additional services. . . . "We've talked with the workers, and they really like the idea a spokesman said. The hurdle will be the employers."
> (*The Carrboro* [NC] *Citizen*, August 16, 2012)

In today's economy the pool of laborers includes maids, housecleaners, and childcare workers, and the employers are not necessarily big landowners but well-off members of the middle class. Where I grew up, the hiring depots were the various union halls spread throughout the metropolitan area. If a contractor was "short a man," he might telephone the hall for an idle hod carrier, iron worker, or laborer, and the man would be sent over for a day's work and a day's paycheck. This is not the best way to make a living, but as Carl Sandberg observes in his poem "Muckers" (1916), even the worst jobs look good when you have no work:

131

Twenty men stand watching the muckers.
   Stabbing the sides of the ditch
   Where clay gleams yellow,
   Driving the blades of the shovels
   Deeper and deeper for the new gas mains,
   Wiping the sweat off their faces
     With red bandanas.
The muckers work on . . . pausing . . . to pull
Their boots out of suckholes where they slosh.

   Of the twenty looking on
Ten murmur, "O, it's a hell of a job,"
Ten others, "Jesus, I wish I had the job."
             (*Chicago Poems*, 8–9)

Bosses and Laborers

Read the parable of the Workers in the Vineyard (Matt. 20:1–16) in the context of unemployment, pickup jobs, and the power imbalance between well-to-do bosses and desperate, expendable laborers, and suddenly a new or more pungent meaning of the parable rises to the surface, one in which theories of the kingdom of heaven and arguments over textual transmission have lost their urgency. Reading the parables of Jesus with the poor, the oppressed, the sick, the incarcerated, and the abused will produce fewer traditional results and a radically altered view of the parables themselves. Such readings will challenge the received wisdom of Jülicher, Dodd, Jeremias, Norman Perrin, Via, and all the rest, who despite the diversity of their methods seek to understand the parables in *theological* terms.

What drives the social, political, ideological, and economic reading of the parables is the conviction that the message of Jesus first took root among the poor. This is a truth so amply attested to in the Gospels that it requires no proof. According to Luke, Jesus has been appointed "to preach good news to the poor" (Luke 4:18). In reference to the Gospel of Mark, Ched Myers makes the case with the boldest of claims:

132   Mark's story of Jesus stands virtually alone among the literary achievements of antiquity for one reason: it is a narrative for and about the common people. The Gospel reflects the daily realities

of disease, poverty, and disenfranchisement that characterized the social existence of first-century Palestine's "other 95%." . . . Throughout the narrative of Jesus' ministry the crowds are there, continually pursuing, interrupting, and prevailing upon him. Jesus' compassion is always first directed toward the importunate masses and their overwhelming needs and demands. . . . [In all its dimensions, the story of Jesus is told] from below.

(Binding the Strong Man, 39–40)

There is no one way of reading with the poor, and there is no "school" of parable interpretation to which everyone who is alert to social and political realities adheres. Reading with the poor begins with the commitment of the interpreter to be with the poor, to listen to them, to participate in their struggles, and where possible to minister to them. Such work does not begin with revolutionary theories but with pastoral identification. In the preface to his *Reading the Bible with the Damned*, Bob Ekblad writes,

For over twenty-five years I have been reading the Bible in foreign places with unlikely reading partners. . . . My primary objective is to present approaches to Scripture reading and spirituality that I have found helpful in my work with outsiders and alienated insiders. . . . The "outsiders" I envision are first and foremost fellow human beings who perceive themselves as condemned to poverty or permanent exclusion, beyond repair, unable to change, in bondage—in short, "damned."

(xiii–xiv)

Reading with the damned entails a conversion from the theological substance of the parable to the social or interpersonal reality portrayed in it—from what (in German) is called its *Sache* (the subject or substance of a thing) to the *Bild* (the imagery or picture contained in the story), or in the terms familiar to British literary criticism, from its *tenor* to its *vehicle*. It is the "picture" that historical-critical interpreters either dispensed with or treated in a manner that indicated its secondary importance. Thus to the theologically minded interpreter, the core of the parable of the Workers in the Vineyard has to with the identity of the early and late workers and the meaning of their relationship in the kingdom. It is often seen as a parable of Jewish and Gentile Christians, or of the Jewish religious establishment versus social outsiders. When the parable is taken as

133

a seamless unity of artistry and theology, however, and not read in "dualistic" fashion (to use Luise Schottroff's expression in *Parables of Jesus*, 2, 90–98), its center of gravity shifts radically to the plight of those who cry, "No one has hired us." "Jesus, I wish I had the job."

An economic reading of the Workers in the Vineyard has given rise to intriguing, controversial, and/or problematic interpretations, depending on one's theological and literary understanding of the parables. The early, midday, and late workers are not viewed as allegorical placeholders for historical or theological values, as in so much of the theological tradition; instead, according to socio-contextual critics, their plight of landless destitution represents the occasion for Jesus' true ministry. Both Schottroff and Werner Herzog (*The Parables as Subversive Speech*) focus on the economic and political situation that produced the surplus of laborers, or "expendables," whose economic status fell below that of peasants and even slaves. As more and more productive land was concentrated into the hands of fewer and richer urban elites, tenant farmers lost their land and could not support their children. The farmers and many of their children were thereby rendered expendable and quickly descended to subsistence farming, day labor, outlaw bands, begging, and death. Expendables were and continue to be a global phenomenon. The seventeenth-century philosopher Thomas Hobbes memorably characterized the lives of such workers in England as "solitary, poor, nasty, brutish and short" (quoted in Herzog, *Parables as Subversive*, 88; cf. 84–96).

The Workers in the Vineyard is divided into two scenes, the hiring and the reckoning. Schottroff and Herzog see the owner's method of payment as an insult to those who worked the whole day. In arbitrarily disregarding the specific contributions of his employees, he transforms both the work and the workers into a mass of undifferentiated labor, over which he exercises absolute control. In Matthew 20:13–15, the landowner singles out a worker, shames him, and sends him on his way, "banned, shunned, blackballed, or blacklisted." The owner's question, "Am I not allowed to do what I choose with what belongs to me?" summarizes the ideology of his class (Herzog, 93–94). One still hears modern-day corporations voicing a similar question, which is not a question at all, but a defiant assertion made in a contract dispute with workers or used to justify a plant closing whose effects will devastate the community. No, the owner is not a generous man.

134

A sociopolitical reading of the parable, then, focuses on economic oppression and makes it the central element of the story. The parable of the Workers in the Vineyard represents a small but vivid slice of first-century social realism. Following Paulo Freire's "pedagogy of the oppressed," Herzog claims that the parables are "codifications" of a social situation, or models, if you will, of "the way things are" in the economic and social milieu of first-century Palestine. The plots depict codifications of perennial oppression; the characters are not real people but represent the social roles played by the several types of oppressors and the oppressed. The codifications are not merely derived from historical conditions in the time of Jesus; they represent the rules and patterns of many advanced agrarian societies (16–29).

The parables graphically portray the sociopolitical aggregate, which Herzog calls "macro-realism," but they also contain certain unrealistic features. For example, why would the owner himself return repeatedly to the marketplace to hire the workers instead of sending a steward (who makes only a brief appearance at the reckoning; 20:8 RSV). This detail is as unrealistic as a Middle Eastern father running down the road to embrace a disrespectful boy. The landowner's large presence is explained by the necessity of bringing the two codified roles onto the stage to confront each other: the despotic owner and the expendable worker. Together, according to Herzog, they symbolize the reality of the social situation. Of course, one could just as easily explain the owner's appearance in theological terms. Theologically and dramatically, it is necessary to bring God, and not a surrogate, into dialogue with those he has called into the vineyard.

How are we to align the economic situation as codified in the parable and the theological symbol, the kingdom of heaven? Here I find myself sympathetic to Herzog's concern for social realism but unable to follow his atheological conclusions. Must they be at odds with each other? According to Herzog, the reference to the kingdom of heaven at the beginning of the parable is either a Matthean invention, which he says is most likely, or an ironic contrast between God's justice and the high-handed tyranny of the landowner (*Parables as Subversive*, 97). He dismisses the conclusions of Jülicher, Dodd, and Jeremias, who take the parables to be expressions of theology with special reference to the kingdom of God. Such scholarship has produced what Herzog terms "idealist"

135

readings of the parables, with scant regard for their "materialist" settings. The existentialist approach of Dan O. Via and the linguistic theories of Robert Funk and Dominic Crossan fall under the same critique. For "the notion that language, even the language of Jesus, once lived as part of a social, political, economic system, which gave it birth and provided its resonance, was foreign to the enterprise of interpreting the parables." Thus it goes without saying that Herzog rejects the importance of reading the parables in the context of the Gospel narratives, for the evangelists were the first offenders in this regard, selectively investing their accounts with theological and ethical meanings consistent with their larger themes and concerns (*Parables as Subversive*, 13 and 11, closely following Herzog's language). It is not merely interesting or occasionally illuminating to imagine the parables in their precanonical form, but it is absolutely imperative. If this is not done, we are left with what Schottroff in a similar discussion refers to as an "ecclesiological reading" of the parables, that is, one in which dogmatic and ecclesial concerns trump the social issues originally addressed by Jesus (*Parables of Jesus*, 217).

What Herzog seems to imply is nothing less than a theopoetic conspiracy on the part of the evangelists and the entire ecclesial tradition that followed, one that systematically spiritualized Jesus' social concerns and inserted the theological symbol "kingdom of God" or "kingdom of heaven" as cover for Jesus' revolutionary agenda. Yet why Herzog (or others) would view the phrase "kingdom of God" as a later insertion is puzzling, given the potential for political critique inherent in the very word "reign" or "kingdom." One does not stage a triumphantly humble entrance into the capital, enter the central religious complex, and attack its economic symbol without wishing to engage the polis with a radically new performance of the kingdom of God. What is the real revolution?

Herzog's reading eliminates the Gospels' portrait of Jesus as a teller of parables, for *parabolē* as comparison, riddle, figure of speech, or metaphor, attested to throughout the Old Testament and the Gospels, is no longer relevant to an understanding of Jesus. If there is no *kingdom of God*, it cannot be the object of a comparison; nor can it be a powerful, divine intervention in human affairs. If there is no *heaven* to call earth into question, the taut dynamic between the two is deflated. Likewise, the portrait of Jesus as a teacher of wisdom, made popular by Marcus Borg and Dominic

Crossan, does not hold up under scrutiny either, for in that view the only transformation proposed by Jesus occurs in the changed consciousness of his hearers.

In other terms, if a parable consists of its *sense*, which is what happens and is said in the story, and its *reference*, which is the significance to which the sense refers, Herzog's reading collapses the two. If the sense points to nothing apart from itself, *reference* is absorbed into *sense*. But the sense is not the referent. Jesus stories are filled with virgins, judges, widows, slaves, hidden treasure, wheat fields, and fish in the sea. Yet from all indications in the text, his stories are not *about* these things, but about something *other* that is found in and among and beyond them.

According to sociological interpretation, the parables in their original form were not metaphors or allegories but political tracts for the times, presenting scenarios of injustice within the existing social order. They were never meant to suggest spiritual transformation, but to expose a social or economic situation. Such an approach sweeps aside many concerns of traditional parable interpretation, but by disregarding the nature of parable itself, it creates a literary dead end. In Herzog's reading of the parable of the Workers in the Vineyard, for example, the "point" of the story fails to appear. Although the parable itself features stylized characters, dialogue, and a surprising climax, Herzog's reading of the story yields surprisingly little. As Arland Hultgren says of Herzog's political interpretation, "But all this is to ruin a good story" (*Parables of Jesus*, 40). Herzog eliminates as unimportant the real conflict in the parable, which is the tension between the early and late workers; it offers no meaningful comments on the owner's reinterpretation of generosity; it ignores the story's function within the Gospel of Matthew; it effectively severs the story about a vineyard from its antecedents in the Old Testament. All that remains is a "codification" of an unjust situation in Judea.

What is lacking in Herzog's proposal is proof—either from extrabiblical sources or the biblical text itself—that would override or dissolve the linkage of Jesus and the kingdom of God. If Herzog is right, it is not difficult to imagine the motive for the tradition's reinvention of Jesus, for, after all, Rome was a fearsome antagonist, and the Jesus community was living in the belly of the beast. 137
What *does* defy explanation, however, is how the entire Jesus tradition could have agreed upon and executed so thoroughgoing a

transformation of the Lord's identity and mission, and how in the space of a half generation it was able to reinvent the radical political critic as a preacher of the kingdom of heaven.

Herzog does not attempt to "prove" his theory of the parables, and despite the wealth of social theory he brings to his reading of them, his language is not analytic. If it were, he would merely be replicating the historical, critical, and literary language of interpretation with which he finds fault. I read Herzog's work as a provocation. His is the language of proposal, not proof; like a signal flare beside a dangerous stretch of road, his work means to call attention to massive critical insensitivity to a neglected dimension of Jesus' ministry and its political setting. With this in mind, a further question presents itself: If we want to benefit from the sociopolitical reading of the parables, is it necessary to accept Herzog's entire interpretive framework? If not, what are our alternatives?

Luise Schottroff shares most of Herzog's concerns for the sociopolitical background of the parables. She too condemns the landowner's behavior as the antithesis of God's justice. When the owner claims the right to do with his property as he sees fit, she reminds us that such a claim violates the Torah, which teaches that God is the owner of the land. When the owner hires workers at various times in the day, she does not see this as his desire to provide work in the vineyard, but as the owner's manipulation of the labor pool to his own advantage. Therefore the figure of the landowner has no poetic or allegorical association with God.

Unlike Herzog, she makes these judgments within the narrative framework of the Gospels, for she understands that the only hope of achieving a responsible interpretation of any passage requires that it be read in its literary context. This decision allows her to maintain a theological position vis-à-vis the parable. In place of an ideological reading of the parable, she proposes an eschatological one. By eschatology she does not refer to a mythic end time, but the intervention of God into every situation of oppression and injustice. Her reading of the parables represents the sociopolitical version of Dodd's realized eschatology. Instead of collapsing the temporal framework of Jesus' proclamation and reading everything future as present tense, Schottroff translates everything theological into a radical critique of material realities. The coming of Jesus changes everything—now. His claim on us invalidates the old ways of evaluation and domination: in or out, higher or lower, orthodox or heterodox, male or female, gay

138

or straight. Hers is an eschatology of liberation, and she finds clues to that liberation scattered throughout Matthew's Gospel—in the Beatitudes and Jesus' teaching on discipleship and in his saying about the first and the last in Matthew 20:16—but emphatically *not* in the parable of the Workers in the Vineyard. Thus, like Herzog, she is left with an economic situation, but not a story of redemptive inclusion.

If the language of Herzog's interpretation is provocation, Schottroff's language is prayer. She understands that an eschatological vision in which hierarchy and domination are suspended deserves a language other than that of theological argument. Bonhoeffer was grasping at the same intuition when he dreamed of a "new language" as shocking and liberating as the language of Jesus. Just as Jesus conceived new expressions of God's reign, Schottroff (and Bonhoeffer) rightly leads us to the primary language of prayer, which more adequately reflects the immediacy of God and the nearness of the dawning kingdom.

The uncontested value of reading the parables with the poor is twofold: first, it reminds us that Jesus' stories are set against a backdrop of economic and political oppression. Their setting is not mere scenery, however, for the parables originally intended to speak to and against systems of oppression. Ched Myers challenges theologians and preachers to learn social theory and to practice "ideological literacy" as a part of their exegetical vocation and to do so "from the perspective of the gospel." The interpreter does not begin from a social theory, however, but with a rereading of the Jesus stories themselves. Instead of domesticating them into accounts that neatly fit our notions of "Jesus" or "church," we must submit ourselves to their "absolutely subversive character." Obviously, it is easier to apply literary criteria to the parables than sociological critique, for a parable is a literary artifact to which the reader has direct access. With sociological exegesis, on the other hand, one is forever reading between the lines and trying to correlate social and political suspicions about the text with historical conditions or the laws of advanced agrarian societies (Myers, *Binding the Strong Man*, 21, 21–31). Second, reading with the poor reminds us that we are not their benefactors but their partners in hope and action. The best way to read the parables, then, is not in an academic setting or even from a canopied pulpit, but in the context of a Jesus-like ministry.   139

Despite its great value, the social, political, or economic reading of the parables often *mis*reads the nature of theological metaphor and therefore of parable itself. The data gleaned from the study of advanced agrarian economies teaches us a great deal about the setting of Jesus' parables. But the same data may obstruct the theological work of interpretation. If the parables are codifications of a social situation in Israel, they are also theological codifications composed of the elements broadly constitutive of Jesus' mission and the church's life. What are these elements? They fluctuate from parable to parable and even from Gospel to Gospel. In Matthew 20:1–16 they are God, early followers, latecomers, surprise, tension, and a new form of justice that has come to be known as "grace." Reading with the poor does not entail discarding the parable's theological codification in favor of its sociopolitical implications. It is to bring out something new from the interaction of the two.

Ironically, what appears to be an obvious *injustice* to academic readers of the Workers in the Vineyard is deemed *just* by those whose lives have been harshly affected by injustice and economic oppression. Every Sunday morning in Solentiname, a remote archipelago on Lake Nicaragua, the formal sermon was replaced by a group discussion of the appointed Gospel led by the priest and Marxist, Ernesto Cardenal. In *The Gospel in Solentiname*, Cardenal narrates the content of these discussions. The group appears to understand that a parable demands a comparison and that certain details of the story, while relevant, point beyond themselves. It is interesting to observe how the discussants do not allow the politically objectionable features of a story to negate its gracious impact on their lives. They also demonstrate an intuitive grasp of the difference between sense and reference (see above). In their discussion of Matthew 20:1–16, one of the participants says, "He [the landowner] says he has the right to do what he wants with his money, and that's false, because that money didn't belong to him, it belonged to the workers. *But what we're discussing here isn't workers and bosses but the kingdom of God*" (*Solentiname*, 3:180–81, emphasis added). The agricultural workers approve of the parable because it proclaims something they have been yearning for their whole life: radical equality.

MANUEL: It wasn't unjust. Because, hell, it's like if a boss says to me: "Come and work," and afterwards he sees Felipe and he says to him: "You come, too," and Felipe says: "No, it's too late and I'm going to be earning very little." And he says to him: "No, man, why, I'm going to pay you well." And he goes. He's not taking anything from me, it's a favor that he's doing him.

Bosco: And it seems to me that when you make a revolution, the first ones that work in it shouldn't demand more than the others who join it at the end. Because the revolution is equality. It makes everybody the same.

The poor in the village are able to accept the owner's generosity, and they hope for the day when "the last will be first, and the first will be last." They unflinchingly embrace the social realism of the parable, recognizing better than their American counterparts its codification of an oppressive system, but they do so without discarding its promise of radical grace.

Who Owns the Vineyard?

We encounter a second arena of socioeconomic conflict in the parable of the Wicked Tenants, an agricultural parable whose explicit allusions to the vineyard imagery of Isaiah 5, the mission of the prophets, and the murder of the "beloved son" serve as allegorical markers of the fate of Jesus and the church's understanding of it (Matt. 21:33–46 and pars.; see chaps. 2–3 above). What happens, however, when we read the story with its allegorical elements bracketed out? Behind its recital of salvation history and its high Christology, which are undeniable elements in the canonical parable, some interpreters have discerned a more basic story drawn from the earthly ministry and social milieu of Jesus. In this reading, the parable reflects a young prophet's radical opposition to the religious authorities who have usurped and abused the "vineyard." While not an allegory, the vineyard is a metaphor of the religious oppression carried out by the temple authorities who in all three Synoptic contexts are the addressees of the story.

A second, less figurative approach removes the parable from its religious orbit entirely and reads it as a story of socioeconomic exploitation, not unlike that of the parable of the Workers in the Vineyard (Matt. 20:1–16). In this version, it is the absentee landlord 141 who is the villain, and the oppressed tenants who are the victims. Their only crime is to claim their rights to the land as guaranteed in the Torah. A situation so flagrantly unjust is bound to lead to violence, but it is a violence born of desperation, whose seeds have been sown by the rich owner, who, according to William Herzog, has expropriated the peasants' land and turned it into a vineyard. There is nothing more important to workers than the land itself. From the Americas to Africa to Asia, subsistence farmers and tenants who are desperate to feed their families are fighting for one thing: land.

In Herzog's reading, however, one cannot escape the feeling that an enormous superstructure of social theory has been erected on a small religious allegory. No one can deny that large, often foreign landholding elites are gobbling up the land of the poor, but in none of three Synoptic versions of the story is the "man" accused of exploitation. Indeed, in the *Gospel of Thomas*'s version of the story, the owner of the vineyard is called "good" (Funk, Scott, and Butts, *Parables of Jesus*, 51; *Gospel of Thomas* 65). Simply put, the owner sends his beloved son to reclaim what is rightfully his, and the son pays a terrible price for it. Once again, when treated as a codification (or literary model) of social injustice, the parable as we have it in the Gospels loses its point (see the counterarguments of Schottroff, *Parables of Jesus*, 13–28; Herzog, *Parables as Subversive*, 98–113, esp. 104).

We must find a way to recognize the very real social dimension of Jesus' parables without relinquishing the equally real dimension of the kingdom of God that he proclaimed. The sociopolitical contextualization of this and other parables of Jesus raises several fundamental questions: in such comprehensive reconstructions of the parable and its sociopolitical background, can we say that we are still reading the *text*? What is the authority of the text relative to the "laws" of political science and the political commitments we bring to our interpretation of the text? And how do we protect against our own religious commitments when interpreting the parables? That is, if we focus exclusively on the theological dimension of the good news, how do we guard against the easy spiritualization that overlooks the suffering of the poor?

Parabolic Slaves

Similar questions emerge in a consideration of slaves in the parables of Jesus. The world of slavery pervades the stories he told. Seven or possibly eight of Luke's parables (depending on the status of the Dishonest Steward) feature plots and imagery related to slavery. One New Testament scholar characterizes the Jesus of the parables as having an insider's knowledge of slavery and goes so far as to surmise that he himself might have been a former slave (Jennifer Glancy rejects this view in *Slavery in Early Christianity*, 127–28). Slavery is allowed in the Torah; yet the question remains: How is it possible that Jesus can inscribe upon his stories the reality of slavery without commenting on its inherent injustice or the suffering it produces? The question gains poignancy when one remembers that slaves were undoubtedly present in the communities that received these stories and in the assemblies where they were read. The three parables presented in Luke 12:35–48 have as their theme the importance of watchfulness: "You also must be ready, for the Son of Man is coming at an unexpected hour" (Luke 12:40). In two of the three parables, that readiness is defined by the behavior of slaves, both good and bad.

In the first (vv. 37–38), the master is so pleased with his slaves' preparedness that he changes places with them and serves them at table. Of these, Jesus says, "Blessed are those slaves."

In the third and longest of the three parables (vv. 41–48), the slave/manager pays the ultimate price for his lack of preparedness. Jesus says that when the master returns and finds his house in drunken chaos, the slave/manager most responsible will be cut in pieces, and the rest of the slaves will receive a beating. As Luise Schottroff points out, the degrees of punishment and even the impulsive kindness of the master toward the faithful slaves in 12:37–38 cannot conceal the absolute dominion exercised by the owner over his property. The kenotic Jesus, who "humbled himself" at every turn, must not be correlated with the capricious, absentee master in several of the parables, nor with the dominators of the poor throughout human history. She discerns a fundamental conflict between the Jesus of the Gospels (and Paul) and the "master" depicted in the parables of Jesus as they were reformulated by the church (*Parables of Jesus*, 171).

In the parable of the Slave in Luke 17:7–10, we are confronted by an even more desolate picture of the master-slave relationship. Karl Marx once accused the Christian religion of playing a compensatory and illusory role in human society. In his famous comment describing religion as "the opium of the people," he caricatures

143

religion as "the heart of a heartless world" (*On Religion*, 42, emphasis omitted). What we find in Luke 17 is a codification of the harsh world of a petit bourgeois landowner and his one, solitary slave, who must do double-duty as a field hand by day and a house slave and cook by night. These two "flat" characters are locked in an intimate master-slave relationship that does not include friendship, kindness, or civility. Marx's theory notwithstanding, the "heart" in this heartless world is nowhere to be found, not even in Luke's Gospel. The parable offers no hint of gratitude or respect, no aura of spirituality, and no clue to the presence of God. Jesus addresses his little story to a slaveholding audience with the words, "Who among you would say to your slave . . . ?" The ancient world understood the chains of restriction and cruelty that separated a slave from a free person. Every slave's devotion was the by-product of the fear of corporal punishment (Glancy, *Slavery in Early Christianity*, 118).

The severity of the parable stands in sharp contrast to the modern habit of personalizing master-slave relationships with a veneer of cordiality. We pretend that the waiter is not paid to be friendly and really wants to know if we had a good dining experience. We answer with a smile and a tip. We pretend that the man who trims our lawn and the woman who cleans our home really are "like family," even though we have never sat down with them and enjoyed a meal or made a genuine effort to get to know them. We insist that in a democratic society we are all on an equal footing, and that the poorest and least educated among us has as good a chance as anyone else of becoming president. What is true of the world of the waiter, worker, and maid applies also to the hairdresser, garage mechanic, grocery clerk, and flight attendant. Who among us will say to any of them, "Why don't you sit down and rest? Let me help you." Jesus is codifying not only his social world, but ours as well.

"Do you thank the slave for doing what was commanded?" (Luke 17:9). It is a heartless little story that Jesus tells because everyone deserves to be thanked and rewarded for their hard work. If there are no rewards, why stay late at the office or in the shop? Why go into debt to send your child to the best university if you cannot expect a payoff down the line? When she joins the premier firm in the city, is it only a parental fantasy that she will say, "Dad, Mom, you made this possible. Thank you!"?

144

Even in so small a story, there is a dramatic shift. For the first three-quarters of the parable, the listeners—that is, you and I—are cast in the role of the master. Who among *us* would offer thanks and respect to our social inferiors? In the last verse, however, the story turns on its tiny axis, and the former subjects of the parable become its objects. "So *you* also, when you have done all that you were ordered to do, say, 'We are worthless slaves; we have done only what we ought to have done!'"

"Hello, my name is Richard. I'll be your server this morning. And when you are sick, I'll kneel beside your hospital bed and pray for you; and when you are sad or angry, I'll sit at your kitchen table and listen; and when you are hungry and thirsty for redemption, I'll meet you at the table and ask, 'Would you like to hear about our specials?' 'The body of Christ given for you, the blood of Christ shed for you.' No need to thank me. It's almost bad form to do so. I am only the servant. It is my duty."

She works for a large home-health company that specializes in physical rehabilitation. Because she is a professional, she is sure to wear her blue scrubs every day as she makes her rounds. She enters the poorest homes and double-wides, teaching the infirm, the disabled, and stroke victims how to get dressed, make their beds, and cook breakfast. Sometimes she finds herself cleaning up messes, even though she is a professional. She is always on her own. There is no audience to admire her virtue. She hears no cosmic applause. She will not write a book about her "ministry." Even her clients do not always express their gratitude. She does good works in a silent and unresponsive universe. She is not like so many in Jesus' day, and ours, who are willing to do good works in exchange for public acclaim. In her own quiet way, she has broken through the performance-reward syndrome to the integrity of the work itself.

Of all the offensive material in this parable, the greatest offense may be the Greek phrase "what we ought to have done" (Luke 17:10), which the RSV mercilessly condenses into "our duty." The parable makes a simple comparison: Just as a slave obeys the master out of duty, with no expectation of reward, it is the duty of disciples to obey Jesus without expectation of reward. The explicitly christocentric assertion in the second clause of the comparison, however, is largely unstated, leaving it to the reader to correlate the two sorts of slavery and two sorts of duty. The two emotions that would be expected in any modern account of service are stripped away: the motivation of love and the reward for performance. With these gone, all that remains in this story is the stark reality of obedience.

145

Other passages in the Gospel qualify the harshness of both the social and theological realities depicted in this parable. "A disciple is not above the teacher," Jesus says in Luke 6:40. The servant of Christ cannot expect to be elevated above the master, nor to be given a reward beyond that received by the Lord, who took the form of a slave and became obedient to the point of death (Phil. 2:7–8). The paradox of the Christian faith—taught elsewhere in the Gospels but not in this parable—is that the only way to do your duty is to ground your obedience in something greater than duty. While that new ground is not made explicit in the Synoptics, the Fourth Gospel discloses the provisional character of "slave" in Christian self-understanding. Jesus tells his disciples, "I do not call you slaves any longer, because the slave does not know what the master is doing; but I have called you friends, because I have made known to you everything I have heard from my Father" (John 15:15, my trans.).

The parable of the Slave in Luke 17 would be unbearable if it pointed to nothing beyond duty. It would be unbearably severe were it not for the one who told it and lived it. He spoke of love, but then did his duty on the cross as if to confirm and enact that love. His love is illustrated in the mirror-reversal of this parable, five chapters earlier in Luke 12:37, in which the master does the unthinkable and serves his slaves at table.

From all that has been said, two conclusions are inescapable. First, the Christian "slave" is not identical with the vast and sad array of the world's slaves, vulnerable people who are subject to a master's capriciousness and cruelty. God does not torment his followers. Thus Christian men, women, and children who find themselves in oppressive situations of violence, injustice, sexual servitude, or domestic abuse should not be counseled to "do their duty" and remain subservient. Obedience to Jesus should never be used as a tool of social, political, or personal oppression.

Second, it is impossible to read slavery and slaves *out* of this and other parables of Jesus without bowdlerizing the text. The parables of preparedness in Luke 12 make no sense without the slaves who are commanded to remain watchful. Indeed, the characters' status as slaves contributes a metaphoric correspondence to Christians' self-identification: "We proclaim Jesus Christ as Lord and ourselves as your slaves [*doulous*] for Jesus' sake" (2 Cor. 4:5). It is this rough correspondence that instructs us and makes the story a *parabolē*. But the comparison comes by way of contrast. Jesus and

146

the evangelists do not speak of slaves in order to underwrite the cruel practices of slavery, but to highlight a new and healing form of slavery to which Paul refers as "slaves of righteousness" and being "enslaved to God" (Rom. 6:18, 22). In Mark 10:42–45 Jesus explicitly contrasts the tyranny among the Gentiles with the practices of his followers:

> But it is not so among you; but whoever wishes to become great among you must be your servant [*diakonos*], and whoever wishes to be first among you must be slave [*doulos*] of all. For the Son of Man came not to be served but to serve, and to give his life a ransom for many.
>
> (vv. 43–45)

The social reality of slavery was everywhere in Jesus' world. Perhaps that is why it became his linguistic point of transfer from bondage to a new way of life.

The parable of the Slave in Luke 17 makes no sense if we view it only as a socioeconomic codification. The theological application found in verse 10 uses the brutal intimacy depicted in verses 7–9 as a platform upon which to teach the kingdom virtues of selflessness, duty, and unstinting obedience. "We are worthless slaves" was a hard but true saying in the social world of the first century. It is an even harder saying in the twenty-first century, with its high estimate of the *worth* of each person. How can we hear such a word without dismissing it out of hand?

One way is to recognize, again, the essential nature of a parable. Each parable forms a double helix of two distinct realities. The key to understanding its structure is to recognize its double-stranded nature. The duality of parables does not consist in two separate foci of meaning, like an ellipse; but as in the double helix, a parable intertwines the two realities in such a way that one cannot be separated from the other. The "codifications" about which William Herzog has written are not merely social. They are social *and* theological. Just as Luke 17 codifies a specific model of social power and powerlessness, it also codifies a teaching about life in the kingdom of God, neither of which is particularly attractive. They interpenetrate one another like a double-helical molecule or, to use an ancient theological concept, like the permeation of Christ's human and divine natures. The reader is not licensed to pick the metaphors apart, choosing only those details of the codified world

147

that do not offend modern sensibilities. The mystery of this permeation is heightened in the parables of Jesus, for in them Jesus uses the whole messy sprawl of human life as the canvas for God's reign in the world. To eliminate words like "slave," "worthless," "owner," "torturers," or "duty" from Jesus' message runs the risk of a docetic reading (denying the reality)—not of Jesus, but of the world in which he lived and died. By acknowledging such realities in the parable, we allow the divine metaphor to do its work—with disturbing, surprising, and often redemptive results.

Who was Jesus? What did he set out to do? From a social and political perspective, the answer remains unfocused and theoretical because, if Jesus was the political figure some have imagined him to be, the Gospels provide no picture of a corresponding political organization or movement. Indeed, much of what he said about self-denial, nonretaliation, love of enemies, and the elusiveness of the kingdom does not match the profile of a social or political reformer, much less a revolutionary. As a result, some New Testament scholars have been left to theorize a social role for Jesus by associating his message with agrarian and political movements of his day and later periods. Their efforts lend a suggestive but speculative cast both to his person and the early communities founded in his name.

We are not without a witness, however, to the nature of the Jesus community. In Luke's portrait of it in the book of Acts, the movement, or "the Way," turns out to be far more innovative and revolutionary than any of the revolutionary movements that preceded or came after it. Luke portrays the new community both as a continuation of Jesus' earthly ministry and, by the power of the Holy Spirit, a transformation of it. The new community breaks bread together at a common table, at which it remembers the risen Jesus and awaits his return. Its members read Scripture together, now supplemented by testimonies to the words and deeds of the Lord. The movement admits all into its ranks, but the fellowship is drawn primarily from the common people. The community lives nonviolently, practicing the love and forgiveness imparted by the Master. It cares for the poor in its midst and lives in peace with the world, even with those who persecute it and visit it with suffering. Behold, Luke says: the Jesus Revolution.

148

Luke's portrait is itself a memory, and an idealized one at that. But his account allows us to read *back* from the new and innovative

community he describes to the One whose ministry, death, and resurrection made such an ideal possible. In our search for Jesus and
the meaning of his parables, we discover the most likely setting for
their interpretation, the church in all its guises and permutations.
There we open the Scripture and join a host of fellow readers identified in the Bible and the long, living tradition as "the saints."

CHAPTER 6

Reading the Parables
with the Saints

In Book 6 of *The Confessions*, Augustine tells how one day he and his friends came upon the great bishop Ambrose; he was alone and reading silently. They sat for a while watching in amazement, then quietly tiptoed away. To be a bishop in Milan was to be accessible to the people at all times and without appointment; reading alone, to say nothing of reading without making a sound, was not the norm in the ancient world as it is in ours. To read was to read *with*.

The persons and interpretations discussed in this book are the products of reading communities. In their own manner and time, the members of these communities met Jesus by reading his parables. That their readings differ from one another, and sometimes radically so, does not mean that the church is hopelessly divided in its understanding of Scripture. What we might think of as unbridled diversity, or just plain confusion, our predecessors would have welcomed as abundance. Such abundance has always been a mark of the church.

Something of that plenitude may be seen in the following six distinct readings of the parable of the Good Samaritan. None of the readings below qualifies as idiosyncratic, only distinct, and each reading stands for scores of others in kindred interpretive traditions. In its own fashion each is faithful to the word of God and to the demands of its historical context, whether fifth-century Hippo Regius or twentieth-century Atlanta. Each approaches the

151

Scripture as a living word, which, because it is given by the Holy Spirit, enjoys what Irenaeus called the gift of "perpetual youth." We will read with these and all the saints as we always do, in gratitude for their guidance, awed by the tenacity of their engagement with Scripture, and in freedom to build on their insights.

Augustine

Many times Augustine commented on the parable of the Good Samaritan, but not always from the same hermeneutical perspective or with the same conclusions. In some passages he treats it as a demonstration of the universality of Christian love. In these instances his interpretation resembles the category we have termed "example story." In most others, however, he engages the parable with a thoroughly christological reading, an interpretive strategy he learned from Ambrose, Origen, and Irenaeus, and one that continued throughout the Middle Ages. In this reading, the Samaritan is Christ, who in mercy came down from heaven, became our neighbor, and healed the wounds of the human race. Augustine reads the parable allegorically: its every detail is *significant* but never *superfluous* to Christ's redemptive act (Teske, "Good Samaritan," 347–48; Wailes, *Medieval Allegories*, 209–14).

The Samaritan does not "stand for" Jesus. Jesus *is* the Samaritan. "Samaritan" means "guardian" or "protector," and what else does the whole Gospel teach but that Jesus is our guardian and protector? Thus in Augustine's reading, Jesus inhabits the story, takes it over, and dictates its true meaning. Jesus is our true neighbor: just as the Samaritan must come down the road from Jerusalem to Jericho to find the wounded man, so in the incarnation Jesus comes down to us, not only dressing our wounds but also making them his own.

Once the christological coordinate is established, the details of the story fall into place. The man who fell among thieves is not an individual, but Adam, our fallen race, for *in genere humano* (as humans) we are all Adam. The robbers are the sins devised and prompted by the evil one; the traveler is half dead, which indicates that he is partially able to know his Rescuer even though he is wounded by his sins. The priest and the Levite signify the ministries of the old dispensation; the Samaritan's promised return

152

points to events that will occur on the last day. The beast stands for the flesh of Christ; the inn equals the church; the innkeeper is the apostle Paul (Augustine, *Quaestiones evangeliorum* 2.19; Teske, "Good Samaritan," 352, citing many other references). We are only scratching the surface of all that Augustine and the tradition, both before and after him, discovered in the parable. His interpretation offers a splendid example of the ancient and medieval church's understanding of Scripture as a thesaurus of riches.

In other works, such as book 12 of his *Confessions* and book 1 of *On Christian Teaching*, Augustine acknowledges that not everyone will approve of his exegesis. In fact, he reminds his readers that allegory violates his own preference, which is to seek the sacred author's intended meaning of the passage. He is convinced, however, that the christological reading of the Good Samaritan *is* the divine author's intended reading. He might have gone further to insist that Luke's actual intention in writing is far less certain than the catholic truths enumerated in the parable of the Good Samaritan (Teske, "Good Samaritan," 355). More important than the author's intention is the Holy Spirit's purpose in giving us this passage.

Thus for Augustine the issue is not truth versus falsity, but several truths in service of a larger truth. As long as the interpreter remains within the bounds of that larger truth, he cannot issue a false reading of a biblical text. It is possible, he says, to miss the writer's intention but faithfully to teach the love of God anyway, much in the way a hiker can leave the path and still reach his destination by cutting through a field.

Augustine draws his theological hermeneutic from the verses immediately preceding the parable of the Good Samaritan: "You shall love the Lord your God with all your heart, and with all your soul, and with all your mind; and your neighbor as yourself" (Luke 10:27). He writes,

> So anyone who thinks that he has understood the divine Scriptures or any part of them, but cannot by his understanding build up this double love of God and neighbor, has not yet succeeded in understanding them. Anyone who derives from them an idea which is useful for supporting this love but fails to say what the writer demonstrably meant in the passage has not made a fatal error, and is certainly not a liar.
> (*On Christian Teaching* 1.86; cf. 1.87–88)

Writing in a different genre and a different age, the American poet e. e. cummings addresses the same question posed by Augustine: What is the focus of the parable of the Good Samaritan? Who is the Samaritan? In the title of his poem on Luke 10:25–37, "A Man Who Had Fallen among Thieves" (1926), the poet gives his provisional answer. He will read this story through the *victim's* eyes. The poet will drag us through a "frozen brook / of pinkest vomit" until we experience the banality and sickening vulnerability of the victim. But then, in true parable fashion, the poet will surprise us in the final stanza by switching the focus of the poem entirely. He will suddenly and explicitly speak in the voice of the Samaritan, and he will unveil the Samaritan's true identity: "I put him all into my arms." The first sentence of the last stanza signals a major shift in the narrative. It begins with the only capitalized word in the poem—perhaps the poet's version of Luke's use of the word "But" ("But a Samaritan . . .") in 10:33. As it turns out, the poem is something more than an exhortation to "go and do likewise." For at the end, it records the compassionate testimony of the rescuer, who is none other than Jesus the Samaritan, whom himself will be "banged with terror" and achieve cosmic vindication.

Julian of Norwich

The fourteenth-century mystic and theologian Julian of Norwich treats the parable only allusively in her "Parable of the Servant" found in the Long Text of *Revelations of Divine Love*. Like Augustine's allegorical interpretation of the Good Samaritan, her parable contains the whole story—the ABCs, she calls it—of God's love. A lord and his servant are living together harmoniously when the lord sends his servant on a dangerous mission. In his eagerness to make the journey, the servant falls into a ravine and is badly hurt. He is injured, soiled, and his clothing tattered but, worst of all, Julian says, "he lay *alone*." The lord, who is splendidly handsome of countenance and dressed in a garment of azure blue, Julian identifies as God. Following Augustine's allegory, she identifies the servant who falls into the ravine as Adam, "for in the sight of God all men are one."

154

Julian then proceeds to makes a further move that changes the dynamic of the parable. The servant who has fallen is also "the Son,

Jesus Christ," the second person of the Trinity. No longer is Jesus the Samaritan or the guardian, as in Augustine, for in his total identification with the fallen race of Adam, he is to be located in the abject suffering of the man in the ravine. Jesus is the man in the ditch. Only one person could have been entrusted with this dangerous mission; hence the significance of the word *alone*. In ministering to his Son, Jesus, and by raising him from the dead, God ministers to the entire human race with endless patience and concern.

Perplexed by the mystery of her own vision, Julian is instructed to pay attention to "all the details and properties that were shown." In that regard, the clothing imagery is essential to her parable. Just as the traveler in Luke is stripped of his clothes, so the servant/Son, who was plainly dressed to begin with, will at the end stand before God in Adam's old clothes, "for Jesus is all who shall be saved, and all who shall be saved are Jesus." Then God will redress him (and us) in the glory of beautiful new clothes more elegant than the Father's.

A further point of contact with the Good Samaritan may be found in the compassion with which the lord rescues his servant Adam/Jesus. Julian uses the phrase "compassion and pity" nineteen times in the parable (Hide, "Parable of the Servant," 58–59; citing Palliser, *Mother of Mercy*, 167). Just as the Samaritan was "moved with pity," bandaged the victim's wounds, and took care of him, so God cares for us in Christ and cares for Christ in us (Julian, *Revelations*, Long Text, 115–24, chap. 51).

Julian's identification of the traveler with Christ is relatively rare among the interpreters of the Good Samaritan. We might take note of a modern example of the same theological reading. In his book *The Parables of Grace*, Robert Capon notices that in Mark and Matthew the question "What is the greatest commandment?" is asked in the context of Passion Week, which leads him to interpret Luke's version of the question, "What must I do to inherit eternal life?" and the parable that follows as intimately related to the passion of Christ (which in Luke it is not). This move allows him to assert that the parable of the Good Samaritan is "about" the passion and resurrection of Jesus. According to Capon, it is not the Samaritan who is the key figure—despite the elaborate description of his acts of goodness, which form the core and climax of the story—but it is the man who fell among thieves. And that man, the man in the parabolic ditch, is Jesus.

What is the role of the Samaritan? In Capon's reading, the Samaritan stands for believers who are called to share in the passion of the man who lies in the ditch (Jesus). The parable is not about imitating the Samaritan's compassionate behavior. The only imitation enjoined in this story is practiced by the believer who participates in the "outcastness" and "lostness" of the man who fell among thieves. His key interpretive move resembles Julian's, but Capon overlooks the rest of the story, including the Lord's command to "Go and do likewise," which several interpreters judge to be a part of the "frame" the evangelist has placed around the story. The command to "do," however, is the mechanism that makes the parable a "story of intent." It echoes Jesus' earlier word to the lawyer: "*Do* this, and you will live" (Luke 10:28, emphasis added). In Capon's reading, we are not commanded to imitate the Samaritan's neighbor love but the Samaritan's "spiritual insight" (*Parables of Grace*, 58–67).

Capon's conclusions honor the crucifixion and resurrection of Jesus. Jesus was indeed rejected and crucified, and to be a Christian is to identify with his suffering, especially during Lent. Yet his reading of the parable fails to acknowledge the obvious importance of the Samaritan, who in Julian's "Parable of the Servant" corresponds to the compassionate, merciful Lord.

When Jesus says, "*But* a Samaritan . . ." (emphasis added), the parable becomes the Samaritan's story. *His* emotional reaction, *his* compassionate behavior, and *his* promise to the innkeeper are all narrated with an enormous density of detail. No ordinary reader can overlook the centrality of the Samaritan in the parable. Everything about it, including Jesus' final comments, point in the same direction: to belong to the kingdom of God means to love the way this man loves. Capon's reading eliminates the response of mercy from the essence of the gospel, which is also the priest's and Levite's mistake. They adhere to their sacred traditions but at the cost of obedience, love, and mercy. Jesus' question is integral to the story (why ask it if not to elicit an answer?): "'Which of these three, do you think, was a neighbor to the man who fell into the hands of the robbers?' He said, 'The one who showed him mercy.' Jesus said to him, 'Go and do likewise.'" On these three sentences hangs the interpretation of the parable.

For once, the lawyer gets it right.

156

Luther

A postil was a sermonic exposition or sample homily designed for use by the clergy. In his introductory remarks to a postil on Luke 10:25–37, Martin Luther addresses himself to the question "Who is my neighbor?" He says that the Lord's parable of the Good Samaritan reveals that we are all neighbors to one another, both those who are in need and those who offer assistance (Luther, *Sermons*, 5:19–35). He does not explore the limiting implication of the lawyer's question (whom may I exclude from the category of "neighbor"?); nor does he comment on Leviticus 19:18, "You shall love your neighbor as yourself," where the neighbor is the fellow Israelite, or 19:34, where the concept is extended to include the resident alien: "You shall love the alien as yourself."

Nor does he probe the wider and more challenging implications of his own phrase, "We are all neighbors." It is clear that Luther's generalization has its limits, too, given the immediate context of this assertion, in which he assails Jews, Catholics, lawyers, and believers in free will. With his introductory observations out of the way, he comes to the heart of his message.

"This Samaritan of course is our Lord Jesus Christ himself" (Luther, *Sermons*, 5:27). With these words Luther picks up the mantle of Augustine and the allegorical method he had years before rejected. Like the Samaritan, Jesus comes uninvited with his ministry of compassion and deliverance. More accurately, Jesus is not *like* the Samaritan; according to Luther, he is "the true Samaritan." This Samaritan offers more than an example for us to follow; rather, Christ's parable provides a pictorial reenactment of our own deliverance. The true Samaritan's act of love "avails for us."

Like Augustine and Julian of Norwich, Luther discerns in this parable "the substance of the gospel." He rejoins the tradition of allegory, which he had earlier criticized, but changes its individual terms to suit the needs of his theological movement. The man in the ditch is Adam, who stands for all humankind. "Half dead" accurately describes the human condition weakened by reliance on reason and good works. The priest signifies the patriarchs before Moses; the Levite passes for the priesthood of the Old Testament. The oil is the balm of the gospel; the wine is "sharp" and represents

157

the holy cross. The beast is Christ himself. The inn is Christianity; the innkeeper is an evangelical preacher.

He adds a further word of application for clergy of the evangelical churches. After voicing the usual complaints against authoritarian priests and bishops, he suggests that the Good Samaritan offers an alternative model for the minister, who "ought to resemble one who waits upon the sick, who treats them very gently, gives kind words, speaks very friendly to them, and exercises all diligence in their behalf." Remember, he says, the parish should be considered a hospital or infirmary for the wounded.

Calvin

In his commentary on the parable of the Good Samaritan, John Calvin wonders why some readers of Scripture think they have the liberty to disguise the natural meaning of the text with their speculative interpretations. What is needed, he says, is a deeper reverence for the Bible.

With regard to the parable, he identifies two allegorical approaches, both of which he rejects. The first is that of the believers in free will, who identify the wounded man with Adam and, further, claim that the phrase "half dead" indicates that the power of acting well was not wholly extinguished in him. As if, he continues, Jesus would tell this parable in order to comment on the capacities of human nature! The second rejected allegory is the more popular of the two. This is the imagined (and spurious) identification of the Samaritan with Christ. It is also claimed that the oil and wine represent repentance and grace and that the innkeeper stands for the church. All such interpretations are wrong.

What is clear to Calvin is that this passage teaches a neighborliness unmatched by our own practices and those of the Jews who "with barbarous and unfeeling contempt . . . despised each other." Calvin comes close to arguing that Jesus teaches this lesson on neighborliness for the purpose of exposing the divisions and hatefulness of his own people. In any case, the parable makes it clear that we are all neighbors, which is an observed truth available to everyone, including us, by virtue of our common humanity.

158

The implication of Calvin's comment is that a parable of Jesus need not be interpreted soteriologically, that is, as an expression of our redemption through Christ. It is sufficient to say that the parable demonstrates the common creation of all people, which is a truth known to natural reason. "To make any person our *neighbor*, therefore, it is enough that he be a man; for it is not in our power to blot out our common nature. . . . The general truth conveyed is that the greatest stranger is *our neighbor*, because God has bound all men together, for the purpose of assisting each other." As in Luther, the interpreter's appreciation of the neighbor stops well short of the Jews and other religious opponents. Thus, while Calvin's approach appears to be the progenitor of modern Good Samaritan laws, premised as they are on brotherhood and a common humanity, its universality is limited in practice by theological considerations (*Commentary on a Harmony*, 3:54–63).

King

The early and medieval church identified four senses by which to read Scripture: the literal, allegorical, eschatological, and moral. These were the gates to the manifold riches of the Bible. Although trained in higher criticism, with its decidedly historical bias, Martin Luther King Jr. was at home in all the senses of biblical interpretation. He preached more sermons on the parables than on any other biblical genre, and in most of them he employed the techniques of allegory. In his sermons on the parable of the Good Samaritan, however, he did not allegorize the many details of the story but sought their *moral* meaning. The plot and characterization in the story suggested topoi, or "sites," from which King proclaimed his moral vision for a divided nation.

Like the traditions represented by Augustine, Julian, Luther, and Calvin, King assumes that the frame of the parable, including the lawyer's question and Jesus' concluding statements, are integral to the parable itself. Early in his 1966 sermon on the passage, King reminds his congregation that Jesus chose the vehicle of *story* to answer the lawyer's question: "Now, you know that question could have very easily ended up in a philosophical and theological debate. But Jesus determined not to get bogged down in the paralysis of analysis. He immediately pulled that question out of thin air and placed it on a dangerous curve between Jerusalem and Jericho." In other words, the story-form itself indicates God's willingness to

159

reach out to us and accommodate his truth to our limited under-standing ("Good Samaritan," transcript, 1966).

In the 1966 sermon, King organizes his thoughts around three "philosophies of life"—the robbers' "What's yours is mine"; the priest's and Levite's "What's mine is mine, and what's yours is yours"; and the Samaritan's philosophy, "What's mine is yours." In other treatments of the story, he alludes to three types of altruism in the Samaritan's behavior. In either case, the headings serve as little more than placeholders, topoi, for King's reading of both the text and the racial crisis in America.

If Julian of Norwich was fixated by the Lord's compassion, it is the subject of race that broods over King's exposition of the Good Samaritan. He is "a man of another race," which in some quarters would rule him out as a neighbor, King says, but a neighbor is any-one in need and anyone willing to help. The neighbor may not be a member of your church, the person next door, or someone of the same color. Jesus seems to say of the neighbor, "I don't know his name." The universal scope of neighborliness resonates perfectly with the vision of race relations King had been preaching for thir-teen years.

In speaking of the robbers' philosophy, he moralizes the text by exploring the many ways racism robs its victims of their dignity, opportunity, and family stability. What began with the great rob-bery of slavery continues today in Atlanta, Birmingham, and Chi-cago in the form of lesser robberies and humiliations carried out on a daily basis.

He sees the priest's and Levite's self-protective philosophy mir-rored in the majority of white preachers, who are "much more cau-tious than courageous," who don't have the guts to take a stand. King is also critical of black church preachers and members of the growing black middle class, who are concerned only for themselves and have forgotten about those left behind.

When he comes to the Good Samaritan's philosophy, "What's mine is yours," he observes that the Samaritan did not practice "compassion by proxy." "I see that man getting down from his beast. . . . You know a lot of people pity folk. And they'll send a little money here and there. But they don't truly empathize. . . . Pity is feeling sorry for somebody, but empathy is feeling with somebody."

Prompted by the Samaritan's selflessness, King gives his own testimony. It too is consistent with a moral reading of the text: "I choose to identify with the underprivileged. I choose to identify with the poor. . . . If it means sacrificing, I'm going that way. If it means dying for them, I'm going that way" ("Good Samaritan," transcript, 1966).

In February 1968, he preached on the same text under the title "Who Is My Neighbor?" It is essentially the same sermon, but the rhetorical *scene* has shifted from the exclusive focus on race to the growing controversy over Vietnam. In place of the three philosophies outlined in the early sermon, he attributes to the Samaritan three kinds of altruism. The later version is a much more personal sermon. The preacher confesses that he himself once profiled a man asking for help beside a road in his neighborhood; fearing for his own safety, he passed him by. Inspired by the Samaritan's courage, the preacher promises always to stand up for what is right, even though "somebody may shoot at you." The alternative to moral courage is the sort of death that attends the coward, no matter what his age (transcript, 1968).

King preached on the Good Samaritan one last time, the night before he died. In this version, the defining context of the sermon is the striking sanitation workers in Memphis. King asks, "Who will stop for them? The question is not, What will happen to *me* if I stop, but what will happen to *them* if I do not? What is required of us is 'a kind of dangerous unselfishness'" (King, "I See the Promised Land," in *Testament of Hope*, 284–85).

In his every sermon on the Good Samaritan, King interprets the story as guidance for the nation's and the Christian's moral life, for it teaches compassion, courage, and sacrifice, exemplified not only by a character in the story but also by the Christ who died on a cross. From another perspective, however, King echoes the themes of John Crossan and Robert Funk, who have argued that the parable is not a moral lesson in behavior but a metaphor for the unexpected manner in which we receive deliverance. In our discussion of Funk's interpretation of the Good Samaritan in chapter 4, we concluded that the real question the parable seeks to answer may *not* be, "Whom should I help?" but "From whom am I willing to receive help?" King often pointed to the black church's messianic assignment: "To save the soul of the nation." It would be by the black person's compassion, courage, and willingness to suffer that America's sins would be put right with God and history. Who is in the ditch? Is it a Jew? Is it Jesus? No, America lies in the ditch. Will

161

white America be willing to accept its rescue from an unexpected source, from another race, a former enemy—the "other"?

The Men and Women of Solentiname

The informal dialogue of campesinos in an artists' colony on Lake Nicaragua echoes the anger expressed by Luther, Calvin, and King, first at the lawyer's trap question, then at the behavior of the priest and the Levite. Unlike Luther and Calvin, however, their discussion leads to explicitly *political* conclusions. The villagers read the text from a social and political setting very different from academia or the established church. They express their resentment at the priests and leaders of the church who in their view have forsaken the true meaning of the gospel. Claiming to be Christian and spiritual, the authorities have sided with powerful institutions and disregarded the plight of the poor. One says, "It was religion itself that prevented them [the priest and the Levite] from loving their neighbor, and that kind of thing is still going on" (Cardenal, *Solentiname*, 3:94–104).

The participants' critique is couched in the Latin American Marxism of the 1970s, substituting "comrades" for "neighbors" and "comradeship" for love. A neighbor is simply *there* in the same church or class; a comrade is someone you care about, whose struggle you join. One of the group says, "Being charitable to the poor, giving them worn-out clothes, isn't loving your neighbor. Love of your neighbor is comradeship." Another identifies the Good Samaritan as an atheist who cares about the poor.

The leader (Cardenal) notices that the lawyer asks a "dangerous question." It would be as if someone from the corrupt Somoza regime might ask what we think of the gospel. It's a question loaded with political implications. The lawyer clearly wishes to limit the field of those whom he is expected to treat as a neighbor. Jesus answers not with a limiting definition, but by expanding the scope of "neighbor" to include one who acts as a neighbor. Who was the neighbor? One man answers, "It wasn't the wounded man."

In the remainder of the discussion, several members of the group wonder aloud why, after Jesus quotes the two great commands of the law, he illustrates only one of them. Unlike most interpretations, which assume that the first command to love God is the

162

foundation of the second, the group at Solentiname places greater value on the second, the command to love the neighbor. It is easy to go to church and do the spiritual part of religion, but it's much harder to take a stand and care for others. With this, the gathering of campesinos begins to sound like Martin Luther King.

If there is any "solution" to the question of the two command-ments, it comes from a man named Laureano, who formulates a syn-thesis that Julian of Norwich might have approved: "God is all of us who love each other." To which the leader replies, "Saint Augustine says God is the love with which we love each other." A woman named Olivia concludes, "It's hard to be a Christian, like that Samaritan was. It's easier to be just religious" (Cardenal, *Solentiname*, 3:103).

Reading with the saints does not require prerequisites. One need not be familiar with countless theories and methods of inter-pretation. What such reading first evokes is a wider and deeper appreciation of the saints themselves, both famous and anonymous, who have opened the parables of Jesus, read them, and made them-selves accountable to them. The "saints" are a sensualist-turned-bishop, a mystical recluse, a renegade monk, an urbane theologian, a social revolutionary, and a group of villagers who in generations past would have been called "peasants."

Reading with them yields several approaches to interpretation:

1. Augustine reads the story *ecclesially* and *christologically*, as an exposition of the faith of the church. The key figure is the Samar-itan, Jesus Christ, who rescues the wounded man in the ditch.

2. Julian of Norwich reads the parable *mystically* as the revela-tion of Christ's compassionate and mysterious presence in Adam, the human race. For Julian, the key figure is also Jesus, the wounded servant who lies in the ravine.

3. Luther reads the parable *evangelically*, understanding it as the summary of the gospel and a model for a newly constituted ministry.

4. Calvin reads it *didactically*, as a clear exposition of the neigh-borliness of all human beings, which is a truth derived from reason and creation.

5. King reads the parable *morally* and *prophetically*, as a call to commitment in the face of racism and war. Of all the interpret-ers surveyed, he is the only one to read it in light of the kingdom of God.

163

6. The men and women of Solentiname read the parable *politically*, as a commentary on the failures of authoritarian regimes and as a sign of Jesus' love for the poor; and they read it *eschatologically*, in their enduring hope for a better future.

Despite their diversity of readings, the saints surveyed in this chapter contextualize their interpretation by means of worship: following the reading of the parable, each would have joined in the singing of a psalm or a hymn and then gathered at an altar or simple table to meet the risen Lord in the sacrament. Whether in the *Stadtkirche* (town church) in Wittenberg, Ebenezer Baptist Church in Atlanta, or a commune in the Solentiname Islands, these and countless others would have read the parables as Scripture, always in the context of the church's teaching, worship, and sacraments.

Given that commonality, we can entertain radically divergent readings of the parables with an element of trust, and even friendship, which is not usually a feature of academic controversies. We read as brothers and sisters across time and space, which is to say, we read in relationship with people we do not know personally, but with whom we share a common belief and a core set of practices. We read with those to whom we are joined, not by blood, tribe, sect, or theory, but in the body of a divine person.

In the brief summaries above, all the interpretive lenses mentioned in this book are represented. Is it possible to choose a "right" position?

It is not, because the question itself freezes the living history of interpretation and makes of it a tray of options from which the reader may select one (and only one) position, as if one were to say, "I am a structuralist," or "I am a canonical interpreter," or "I am an allegorist." But as the Jewish scholar Meier Sternberg reminds us, the biblical specialists "speak as if there were one Bible for the historian, another for the theologian, another for the linguist, another for the geneticist, still another for the literary critic. But there are not enough Bibles to go around." Yet its language and message remain "indivisible" (Sternberg, *Poetics of Biblical Narrative*, 17). Nor is it adequate to claim that "all of the above" options are right, for such a judgment overlooks linguistic patterns and contextual clues to meaning that are present in the narrative itself and make themselves available to all. A reading may be "right" for its time and place, and all the interpretations we have surveyed may be "in" the story and useful to various reading communities, but the "indivisible" nature of the scriptural text, like the unity of a fractured church or the indivisibility of Jesus himself—remains.

When we read the Scripture, we are joining a conversation that has been going on a long time. The key to our participation is knowing as much as possible about the dialogue that has preceded us. In that way we will not be tempted to mistake the current conversation for the *only* conversation available to us. We read the parables fully aware that they themselves arose in conversation and confrontation. They were evoked by the crisis of the dawning kingdom of God, and therefore they are meant to speak to the crises of every generation of believers. P. T. Forsyth once defined theology as "the gospel taking the age seriously." Biblical interpretation and preaching do the same, the former under the cloak of technical objectivity, the latter openly and unashamedly committed—prejudiced, in the best sense—but neither in a vacuum sealed off from the defining issues and dilemmas of the age.

Like all conversations, this one has been sharpened by disagreements and conflict (Williams, "Literal Sense of Scripture," 128–29). What satisfies one generation or community proves inadequate to others. Since Christians are forbidden to be enemies in the biblical sense, their conflicts of interpretation are never absolute or conclusive, but introductory to the next phase or another module of the conversation: Augustine's ecclesial reading is both accepted and sharply modified by Luther. Luther's allegory is reversed by Calvin, whose cerebral interpretation is overturned by the mystical tradition represented by Julian of Norwich. The spirituality of Augustine, Julian, and Luther is brought to earth by Martin Luther King Jr. and the campesinos in Solentiname. And so it goes, and so it will go until the party comes to an end.

For some, the parables will appear as instructions, confirming truths they have already come to accept; for others, they will be provocations, unsettling the minds and habits of the self-satisfied. We have learned that both functions—instruction and provocation—are present in one and the same story. The challenge of reading in multiple registers belongs to *phronēsis*, or discernment, which is characteristic of pastoral work in general and preaching in particular. *Phronēsis* is discernment in matters that might be otherwise, for which no fixed rules apply. What could offer a more challenging literary arena for such discernment than the interpretation of a parable? This means that one does not approach the text of a parable with a predetermined conclusion or a set method of interpretation in mind. Each parable offers a cast of characters, a plot, a setting, and a variety of theological and literary accents. The contemporary preacher, solidly planted in his or her own age and beset by its problems, carefully listens to the text and chooses those accents most necessary for the sustenance and mission of the present community. From all the source material available in the text and its environment, the preacher or interpreter struggles to discern what Jesus was trying to accomplish with his story and then tries to do the same.

The original and ultimate purpose of the Lord in telling a parable I call *gospel*. For even those parables containing provocative or judgmental words constitute God's move *toward* Israel and, through Israel, to the church and all humanity. They either gesture that movement, as in the parables of the Sower, the Growing Seed, and the Leaven, or they capture it in their entirety, as in the parables of the Workers in the Vineyard, the Wicked Tenants, the Great Feast, and the Prodigal Son.

If we readers remain in conversation with the gospel, then, we join Augustine, Julian, Luther, Calvin, King, our friends in Solentiname, and the whole cloud of witnesses—in heaven and on earth—who have made an interpretive response to God's love in Christ. For all our readings, like theirs, fall under some provision of God's intervention in human affairs through the ministry, death, and resurrection of the Son. And if we remain in conversation with the text and not merely with theories of its interpretation, we will hear the one gospel in its many voices and respond as "doers of the word, and not hearers only" (Jas. 1:22 RSV). Then Jesus' questions will no longer trouble us, as they once accused the lawyer who put him to the test: What is written? How do you read?

BIBLIOGRAPHY

Aristotle. *Poetics*. Translated by Ingram Bywater. New York: Modern Library, 1954.

———. *Rhetoric*. Translated by W. Rhys Roberts. New York: Modern Library, 1954.

Augustine. *The Confessions*. Translated by Maria Boulding, OSB. New York: Vintage Books, 1994.

———. *Essential Sermons*, edited by Boniface Ramsey. Translated by Edmund Hill, OP. Hyde Park, NY: New City Press, 2007.

———. *On Christian Teaching*. Translated by R. P. H. Green. Oxford: Oxford University Press, 1997.

———. *Quaestiones evangeliorum*. Auerelii Augustini opera, part 13.3. Corpus Christianorum: Series latina 44B. Turnhout, Belgium: Brepols, 1980.

Austin, John L. *How to Do Things with Words*. 2nd ed. Cambridge, MA: Harvard University Press, 1962.

Bailey, Kenneth Ewing. *Poet and Peasant: A Literary Cultural Approach to the Parables in Luke*. Grand Rapids: Wm. B. Eerdmans Publishing Co., 1976.

Barnes, Craig. *The Pastor as Minor Poet: Texts and Subtexts in the Ministerial Life*. Grand Rapids: Wm. B. Eerdmans Publishing Co., 2009.

Beardslee, William. "Narrative Form in the New Testament and Process Theology." *Encounter* 36 (1975): 301–15.

Being There. Film, directed by Hal Ashby. Lorimar Film Entertainment, 1979.

Benjamin, Walter. *Illuminations: Essays and Reflections*. Translated by Harry Zohn. German, 1955. New York: Schocken Books, 1968.

Bockmuehl, Markus, "God's Life as a Jew: Remembering the Son of God as Son of David." In *Seeking the Identity of Jesus: A Pilgrimage*, edited by Beverly Roberts Gaventa and Richard B. Hays, 60–78. Grand Rapids: Wm. B. Eerdmans Publishing Co., 2008.

Bonhoeffer, Dietrich. *Letters and Papers from Prison.* Translated by Reginald Fuller et al. New York: Simon & Schuster, 1953.

Borg, Marcus. *Jesus in Contemporary Scholarship.* Valley Forge, PA: Trinity Press International, 1984.

Bradbury, Ray. *Fahrenheit 451.* New York: Random House, 1953.

Bultmann, Rudolf. *The History of the Synoptic Tradition.* Translated by John Marsh. German, 1921. Oxford: Basil Blackwell, 1963.

Calvin, John. *Commentary on a Harmony of the Evangelists, Matthew, Mark, and Luke.* Translated by William Pringle. Vol. 3. Grand Rapids: Wm. B. Eerdmans Publishing Co., 1949.

Capon, Robert Farrar. *The Parables of Grace.* Grand Rapids: Wm. B. Eerdmans Publishing Co., 1988.

Cardenal, Ernesto. *The Gospel in Solentiname.* Translated by Donald D. Walsh. Vol. 3. Maryknoll, NY: Orbis Books, 1979

Craddock, Fred B. *Overhearing the Gospel.* Nashville: Abingdon Press, 1978.

Crossan, John Dominic. *The Dark Interval: Towards a Theology of Story.* Allen, TX: Argus Communications, 1975.

cummings, e. e. *Complete Poems.* Edited by George James Firmage. London: Granada Publishing, 1981.

Davis, Ellen F., and Richard B. Hays, eds. *The Art of Reading Scripture.* Grand Rapids: Wm. B. Eerdmans Publishing Co., 2003.

Dodd, C. H. *The Parables of the Kingdom.* Rev. ed. New York: Charles Scribner's Sons, 1961.

Donahue, John R. *The Gospel in Parable: Metaphor, Narrative, and Theology in the Synoptic Gospels.* Philadelphia: Fortress Press, 1988.

Ekblad, Bob. *Reading the Bible with the Damned.* Louisville, KY: Westminster John Knox Press, 2005.

Eliot, T. S. *Selected Poems.* London: Faber & Faber, 1961.

Evangelical Lutheran Worship. Minneapolis: Augsburg Fortress, 2006.

Flusser, David. "A New Sensitivity in Judaism and the Christian Message." *Harvard Theological Review* 61 (1968): 107–27.

Funk, Robert W. "The Good Samaritan as Metaphor." *Semeia* 2 (1974): 77–81.

———. *Jesus as Precursor.* Edited by William A. Beardslee. Society of Biblical Literature Semeia Supplements. Philadelphia; Fortress Press; Missoula, MT: Scholars Press, 1975.

Funk, Robert W., Bernard Brandon Scott, and James R. Butts. *The Parables of Jesus: Red Letter Edition; A Report of the Jesus Seminar.* Sonoma, CA: Polebridge Press, 1988.

Gaventa, Beverly Roberts, and Richard B. Hays, eds. *Seeking the Identity of Jesus: A Pilgrimage.* Grand Rapids: Wm. B. Eerdmans Publishing Co., 2008.

Glancy, Jennifer. *Slavery in Early Christianity.* Oxford and New York: Oxford University Press, 2002.

The Gospel of Thomas: The Hidden Sayings of Jesus. Translated critical edition by Marvin Meyer, with an interpretation by Harold Bloom. New York: HarperSanFrancisco, 1992.

Hays, Richard B. *The Moral Vision of the New Testament: A Contemporary Introduction to New Testament Ethics.* New York: HarperOne, 1996.

———. "Salvation by Trust? Reading the Bible Faithfully." *Christian Century* 114, no. 7 (1997): 218–23. Reprinted as "A Hermeneutic of Trust," in *The Company of Preachers: Wisdom on Preaching, Augustine to the Present*, edited by Richard Lischer, 265–74. Grand Rapids: Wm. B. Eerdmans Publishing Co., 2002.

Heim, David. "The Gospel in Seven Words." *Christian Century*, September 5, 2012, 20–25.

Herzog, William R., II. *Parables as Subversive Speech: Jesus as Pedagogue of the Oppressed.* Louisville, KY: Westminster/John Knox Press, 1994.

Hide, Kerrie. "The Parable of the Lord and the Servant: A Soteriology for Our Times." *Pacifica* 10 (February 1997): 53–69.

Horsley, Richard A. *Jesus in Context: Power, People, and Performance.* Minneapolis: Fortress Press, 2008.

Hultgren, Arland J. *The Parables of Jesus: A Commentary.* Grand Rapids: Wm. B. Eerdmans Publishing Co., 2000.

Jeremias, Joachim. *The Parables of Jesus.* Translated by S. H. Hooke. 2nd, rev. ed. New York: Charles Scribner's Sons, 1954.

Julian of Norwich. *Revelations of Divine Love.* Translated by Elizabeth Spearing. London: Penguin Books, 1998.

Jülicher, Adolf. *Die Gleichnisreden Jesu.* 2nd ed. Darmstadt: Wissenschaftliche Buchgesellschaft, 1910. Repr., 1963.

Kafka, Franz. *The Basic Kafka.* Introduction by Erich Heller. New York: Pocket Books, 1958. Repr., 1979.

Keith, Chris. *Jesus and Literacy: Scribal Culture and the Teacher from Galilee.* Edited by Mark Goodacre. Library Studies 413. New York: T&T Clark International, 2011.

Kermode, Frank. *The Genesis of Secrecy: On the Interpretation of Narrative.* Cambridge, MA: Harvard University Press, 1979.

Kierkegaard, Søren. *The Parables of Kierkegaard.* Edited by Thomas C. Oden. Princeton: Princeton University Press, 1978.

King, Martin Luther, Jr. "The Good Samaritan." (1966). Typed transcripts of delivered sermons, Martin Luther King Jr. Center for Nonviolent Social Change, Library and Archives, Atlanta.

———. *A Knock at Midnight.* New York: Warner Books, 1998.

———. *A Testament of Hope: The Essential Writings and Speeches of Martin Luther King, Jr.* Edited by James M. Washington. New York: HarperSanFrancisco, 1986.

———. "Who Is My Neighbor?" (1968). Typed transcripts of delivered sermons, Martin Luther King Jr. Center for Nonviolent Social Change, Library and Archives, Atlanta.

Lewis, C. S. "Bluspels and Flalansferes: A Semantic Nightmare." In *Rehabilitations and Other Essays,* 135–44. London: Oxford University Press, 1939.

Lischer, Richard, ed. *The Company of Preachers: Wisdom on Preaching, Augustine to the Present.* Grand Rapids: Wm. B. Eerdmans Publishing Co., 2002.

———. *The End of Words: The Language of Reconciliation in a Culture of Violence.* Grand Rapids: Wm. B. Eerdmans Publishing Co., 2005.

———. *A Theology of Preaching: The Dynamics of the Gospel/* Rev. ed. Durham, NC: Labyrinth Press, 1992.

———. "What Language Shall I Borrow? The Role of Metaphor in Proclamation." *Dialog* 26 (Fall 1987): 281–86.

Luther, Martin. *Lecture on Romans,* translated and edited by Wilhelm Pauck. *The Library of Christian Classics,* Vol. 15. London: SCM Press, 1961.

———. *The Sermons of Martin Luther.* Vol. 5. Grand Rapids: Baker Book House, 1983.

Lyotard, Jean-François. *The Postmodern Condition: A Report on Knowledge.* Translated by Geoff Bennington and Brian Massumi. Minneapolis: University of Minnesota Press, 1979.

Manguel, Alberto. *A History of Reading.* New York: Viking Press, 1996.

Marcus, Joel. *Mark 1–8: A New Translation with Introduction and Commentary*. Anchor Bible 27. New York: Doubleday, 2000.

Marx, Karl. "Contribution to the Critique of Hegel's Philosophy of Right." In *On Religion: Karl Marx and Friedrich Engels*, 41–58. New York: Schocken Books, 1964.

McArthur, Harvey K., and Robert M. Johnston. *They Also Taught in Parables: Rabbinic Parables from the First Centuries of the Christian Era*. Grand Rapids: Academie Books, 1990.

Milbank, John. *The Word Made Strange: Theology, Language, Culture*. Cambridge, MA: Blackwell Publishers, 1997.

Myers, Ched. *Binding the Strong Man: A Political Reading of Mark's Story of Jesus*. Maryknoll, NY: Orbis Books, 1988. Repr., 2008.

Niebuhr, Reinhold. *The Children of Light and the Children of Darkness*. New York: Charles Scribner's Sons, 1944, 1960.

O'Connor, Flannery. "A Temple of the Holy Ghost" (1954). In *A Good Man Is Hard to Find, and Other Stories*. New York: Harcourt, Brace, 1955.

Oldenhage, Tania. *Parables for Our Time: Rereading New Testament Scholarship after the Holocaust*. New York: Oxford University Press, 2002.

Ong, Walter J. *Orality and Literacy: The Technologizing of the Word*. New York: Routledge, 1982.

Orwell, George. "Politics and the English Language." In *Shooting an Elephant and Other Essays*. New York: Harcourt Brace Jovanovich, 1974.

Palliser, Margaret Ann. *Christ, Our Mother of Mercy: Divine Mercy and Compassion in the Theology of the "Shewings" of Julian of Norwich*. New York: Walter de Gruyter, 1992.

Pelikan, Jaroslav. *Luther the Expositor: Introduction to the Reformer's Exegetical Writings; Companion Volume, Luther's Works*. St. Louis: Concordia Publishing House, 1959.

Perrin, Nicholas. *Thomas: The Other Gospel*. Louisville, KY: Westminster John Knox Press, 2007.

Perrin, Norman. *Jesus and the Language of the Kingdom: Symbol and Metaphor in New Testament Interpretation*. Philadelphia: Fortress Press, 1976.

Richards, Ivor Armstrong. *The Philosophy of Rhetoric*. London: Oxford University Press, 1936.

Robinson, Marilynne. *Gilead*. New York: Farrar, Straus & Giroux, 2004.

————. *Home*. New York: Farrar, Straus & Giroux, 2008.

Sandburg, Carl. *Chicago Poems*. New York: Dover Publications, 1994.

Schneiders, Sandra M. *The Revelatory Text: Interpreting the New Testament as Sacred Scripture*. New York: HarperSanFrancisco, 1991.

Scholes, Robert, and Robert Kellogg. *The Nature of Narrative*. New York: Oxford University Press, 1966.

Schottroff, Luise. *The Parables of Jesus*. Translated by Linda M. Maloney. Minneapolis: Fortress Press, 2006.

Scott, Bernard Brandon. *Hear Then the Parable: A Commentary on the Parables of Jesus*. Minneapolis: Fortress Press, 1989.

Sims, Bennett J. *Servanthood: Leadership for the Third Millennium*. Cambridge, MA: Cowley Publications, 1997.

Sittler, Joseph. "The Unjust Steward." In *The Eloquence of Grace: Joseph Sittler and the Preaching Life*, edited by James M. Childs Jr. and Richard Lischer. Eugene, OR: Cascade Books, 2012.

Smith, Charles W. F. *The Jesus of the Parables*. Rev. ed. Cleveland: United Church Press, 1975.

Snodgrass, Klyne. *Stories with Intent: A Comprehensive Guide to the Parables of Jesus*. Grand Rapids: Wm. B. Eerdmans Publishing Co., 2008.

Stein, Robert H. *An Introduction to the Parables of Jesus*. Philadelphia: Westminster Press, 1981.

Steinmetz, David. "The Superiority of Pre-Critical Exegesis." In *The Theological Interpretation of Scripture: Classic and Contemporary*, edited by Stephen E. Fowl, 26–38. Oxford: Blackwell Publishers, 1997.

Stern, David. "Jesus' Parables from the Perspective of Rabbinic Literature: The Example of the Wicked Husbandmen." In *Parable and Story in Judaism and Christianity*, edited by Clemens Thoma and Michael Wyschogrod, 42–80. New York: Paulist Press, 1989.

Sternberg, Meir. *The Poetics of Biblical Narrative: Ideological Literature and the Drama of Reading*. Bloomington: Indiana University Press, 1985.

Talbert, Charles H. *Reading Luke: A Literary and Theology Commentary on the Third Gospel*. New York: Crossroad Publishing Co., 1988.

Taylor, Barbara Brown. "God's Beloved Thief." In *Home by Another Way*, 3–9. Cambridge, MA: Cowley Publications, 1999.

Teske, Roland. "The Good Samaritan (Luke 10:29–37) in Augustine's Exegesis." In *Augustine: Biblical Exegete*, edited by Frederick Van Fleteren and Joseph C. Schnaubelt, OSA, 347–67. New York: Peter Lang Publishing, 2001.

Thielicke, Helmut. *The Waiting Father: Sermons on the Parables of Jesus*. Translated by John W. Doberstein. New York: Harper & Brothers, 1959.

Thoma, Clemens. "Literary and Theological Aspects of the Rabbinic Parables." In *Parable and Story in Judaism and Christianity*, edited by Clemens Thoma and Michael Wyschogrod, 26–41. New York: Paulist Press, 1989.

Via, Dan O., Jr. *The Parables: Their Literary and Existential Dimension*. Philadelphia: Fortress Press, 1967.

Wailes, Stephen L. *Medieval Allegories of Jesus' Parables*. Berkeley: University of California Press, 1987.

Wesley, John. "The Use of Money." In *The Works of John Wesley*, vol. 2, *Sermons II*, edited by Albert C. Outler. Nashville: Abingdon Press, 1985. Cf. http://wesley.nnu.edu/john-wesley/the-sermons-of-john-wesley-1872-edition/sermon-50-the-use-of-money/.

Wilder, Amos. *Theopoetic: Theology and the Religious Imagination*. Philadelphia: Fortress Press, 1976.

Williams, Rowan. "The Literal Sense of Scripture." *Modern Theology* 7, no. 2 (January 1991): 121–34.

INDEX OF ANCIENT SOURCES

177

INDEX OF SUBJECTS

191